Eamonn Molloy
Traversing the Spectrum of Organisational Autonomy

Eamonn Molloy

Traversing the Spectrum of Organisational Autonomy

The Path to Self-Driving Organisations

DE GRUYTER

ISBN 978-3-11-914216-8
ISBN 978-3-11-222223-2 (PDF)
ISBN 978-3-11-222248-5 (EPUB)
DOI https://doi.org/10.1515/9783112222232

Library of Congress Control Number: 2026932531

Bibliographic information published by the Deutsche Nationalbibliothek
The Deutsche Nationalbibliothek lists this publication in the Deutsche Nationalbibliografie;
detailed bibliographic data are available on the Internet at http://dnb.dnb.de.

De Gruyter and Walter de Gruyter GmbH are part of De Gruyter Brill.
www.degruyterbrill.com

Questions about General Product Safety Regulation:
productsafety@degruyterbrill.com

Cover illustration: track5/E+/Getty Images

For Emily, Leonard, and Emma

Acknowledgements

This book is the product of many conversations, challenges, and generous contributions of time and insight. I am extremely grateful to the following people and organisations for their support: The Fellows, Staff, and Students of Pembroke College, University of Oxford. They provided the ideal conditions and resources to undertake this work. I am particularly indebted to my students (Undergraduates, Masters, Executives, and the Major Projects Leadership Academy) for their insights during our discussions and also for their consistent generosity and understanding when tutorials needed to be rescheduled. Dr Shiwen Li, also at Pembroke College, provided inspirational creative input to the figures at short notice. I am also grateful to Professor Robert Eberhart and the excellent faculty and students at The Ahler School of International Business, UCSD, whose constructive comments and rigorous challenges on early presentations of the spectrum concept were invaluable. Special thanks to Claudia Murphy for getting me into Organisation Design back in the day. On a personal note, I extend my sincere gratitude to Sir David Capewell for his constructive challenge, big ideas, and confidence. Roedd fy ffrind a chydweithredwr Dyfan Williams yn ffynhonnell cyngor sylweddol a doethineb cymwysedig o ddechreuad y syniadau a gynhwysir yma. (My friend and collaborator, Dyfan Williams, was a source of sound advice and applied wisdom from the genesis of the ideas contained here.) My biggest thank you to my family for their unconditional support and rather measured excitement about the whole project.

Contents

Part 4: **The Human Interface: Leadership and Action**

Chapter 8
Machine Leadership —— 115

Chapter 9
Leading the Transition: An Executive Playbook —— 126

Chapter 10
Conclusion: The Paradoxes of Organisational Autonomy —— 138

Introduction: The Idea of Self-Driving Organisations

Imagine an organisation – a firm, a government department, a charity or even a large project – that anticipates the ceaseless flux of its environment, adapting its operations, strategies, and even its core architecture with an intelligence and fluidity that seems almost biological. Picture an enterprise where innovation occurs as a natural product of its interconnected systems; where resources flow to opportunities with minimal friction, guided by data and insight; and where human creative potential is focused on high-value, rewarding activity. While this may sound like a pipe dream or utopian science fiction, it is now a real possibility, what I call the Self-Driving Organisation (henceforth SDO). This book is about how we get there, the opportunities and the risks, and how far we have already come.

Jay Galbraith's (2002, p. 2) astute observation that "The organisation is not an end in itself; it is simply a vehicle for accomplishing the strategic tasks of the business" has a lot of mileage in it. We often compare our corporations and governments, despite their impressive scale and scope, to lumbering supertankers. They are powerful, certainly, but slow to alter course, requiring immense time and effort to react to even minor challenges. Many of us have experienced the daily manifestations of this organisational inertia first-hand: interminable, pointless meetings, siloed, asymmetric information, and bureaucratic quicksand that stifles innovation, inhibits change, and demotivates even the brightest minds and most committed workers.

But what if your organisation could operate and behave less like a behemoth supertanker and more like a sleek, intelligent yacht, constantly sensing its changing environment – the shifting needs of its customers and stakeholders, the actions of its competitors and the stability of its supply chains in real time? What if it could process this information instantaneously, make thousands of coordinated micro-adjustments to its course, and chart its path forward with a sophisticated blend of deep intelligence and a clear, evolving purpose? And what if it could do all of this without you, or anyone else?

This is the promise of the SDO: the potential to achieve a step-change in organisational agility, operational efficiency, and systemic resilience. It is about designing, building, and operating organisations that can learn, adapt, and even evolve their core processes with significantly reduced direct human intervention. This book argues that achieving this requires more than just implementing new technology, though this is a major element of it. The really hard part is that it also requires a fundamental rethinking of the relationship between people and machines, and a conscious choice to build organisations that are not only "smart" in their operation of technologies such as Artificial Intelligence (AI) and Machine Learning (ML) among others, but "wise" in their strategic direction and ethical in their behaviour.

From the outset, I wish to be clear that my intention in this book is to affirm the critical importance of human oversight, strategic direction, and ethical judgement. The increasing levels of machine autonomy in our institutions and organisations make these human contributions more vital than ever. That said, I also claim that we have now entered an era in which the logic of *where* and *how* human intellect is applied in our organisations is profoundly changing. This is much more than the direct substitution of human labour with machines, an extension and washing out of Industrial Revolution practices; it is a move towards delegating the higher-level design, governance, and control of complex systems to intelligent, autonomous, non-human agents. As Stephen Barley (2020) notes, we are not witnessing Industrial Revolution 3.0, or 4.0; this is something quite different, it is a control revolution.

In this book, I use the term organisational autonomy to refer to a systemic property, distinct from classical notions of individual human autonomy. My focus is on the capacity of the organisation as an integrated system to function, make decisions, and adapt with significantly reduced direct human operational involvement. An organisation is deemed autonomous if it possesses the right or power of self-government. This implies that it internalises essential functions like monitoring its own performance and managing its own resources, relying on internal mechanisms for validation and control. This systemic self-governance is conceptually distinct from, though potentially complementary to, the autonomy of the individuals who operate within the organisation.

To build on this, a further critical distinction exists between traditional notions of automation and true autonomy (Bradshaw et al., 2013). Automation, a feature of organisations for centuries, typically involves systems performing rigid, predictable functions according to a predefined script or programme. An automated system is a sophisticated tool that executes a specific command. A simple example is a thermostat that turns on the heat at a set temperature. An assembly line robot performing the same weld thousands of times is automated. In each of these cases, the system operates within a tightly defined envelope, and human oversight is required to verify performance against clear, measurable standards.

Autonomy, in contrast, implies a deeper and more consequential level of independence. An autonomous system pursues a goal. It is designed to operate in complex, dynamic, and often unpredictable environments, with the capacity to sense its surroundings, make its own decisions, and adapt its actions to achieve its objectives. It involves a deliberate cession of a degree of direct control by humans, who must place their trust in the system to act appropriately and manage unforeseen circumstances. A smart power grid that predicts energy demand, analyses market pricing, and makes decisions to optimise power routing is exhibiting autonomy. The key difference lies in the ability to handle variability and make adaptive decisions in the face of uncertainty.

The transformation of organisations to higher levels of autonomy is being enabled by a powerful confluence of maturing and converging forces. The exponential growth of AI and ML is providing the cognitive engine for these systems, enabling them to learn from data and make increasingly sophisticated predictions (Agrawal et al. 2018). This is not simply about AI, however. The continuous development of intelligent automation is providing the muscle for executing ever-more-complex physical and digital tasks. The emergence of decentralised technologies like blockchain and smart contracts is offering a new infrastructure for trust and automated governance. And the pervasive connectivity of the Internet of Things (IoT) is creating a global sensory network, allowing organisations to gather real-time data from the physical world at an unprecedented scale (Porter and Heppelmann 2014).

This book is your comprehensive guide to understanding, navigating, and potentially leading this transformation. To do so, the book employs a simple, yet powerful framework developed specifically for this purpose: The Spectrum of Organisational Autonomy (henceforth SOA). Think of it as a detailed map, charting six distinct levels of self-governance, from Level 0, where humans guide every action, to the theoretical horizon of Level 5, where organisations might operate with full autonomy, the apex SDO.

This spectrum serves as an analytical tool – a way to understand the traverse from one level of organisational autonomy to another, surfacing the inherent trade-offs, the technological prerequisites, the evolving human roles, and the opportunities and risks at each stage. It allows its users to ask not only "where are we now?" but also "what is the right level of autonomy for *this* function in *our* specific context?" For example, the optimal level for a creative advertising agency will be vastly different from that of a nuclear power plant. The SOA provides the language and the logic for making these critical strategic choices and investment decisions consciously and deliberately.

This book is written for anyone seeking to comprehend and participate in shaping the future of organisations. For Leaders, Executives, Strategists, and Board Members, it offers a structured framework for making sense of rapid technological change and a practical playbook for navigating the complex personnel and ethical challenges of this transformation. For technologists and innovators, it provides the broader organisational context for situating and understanding the impact of their work. For Policymakers, Regulators, and Legal Professionals, it offers a structured view of a domain fraught with novel challenges that are multiplying at pace. For researchers and students, it provides new lenses for making sense of organisational change in the twenty-first century. And for readers who just happen to be curious about all of this, it will hopefully help to demystify one of the most significant social transformations of our time.

Over the following pages, we will embark on an in-depth exploration of how our organisations are becoming more autonomous. In Part 1, we will lay the foundations by setting out the SOA framework in detail. In Part 2, we will go under the hood to dissect the core technologies enabling this revolution and examine radical new organisational forms like Decentralised Autonomous Organisations (DAOs) and reflect on some of the lessons they exemplify. In Part 3, we will conduct a function-by-function analysis of how every part of a traditional business – from the strategic brain and the human-machine workforce to the critical legal, security, and ethical considerations – is being rewired and recoded across the spectrum. Finally, in Part 4, we will explore the future of machine leadership before turning to actionable guidance with a phased playbook for executives and managers tasked with leading this intricate transition effectively, efficiently, and responsibly. This book is about how we do it.

Part 1: **A New Framework for Autonomy**

Chapter 1
The Spectrum of Organisational Autonomy: A New Lens on Organisations

Overview

This chapter introduces the Spectrum of Organisational Autonomy (SOA), a novel framework designed to navigate the shift towards self-driving organisations. As enterprises grapple with accelerating technological change, older ways of thinking about organisational structure and control begin to creak. This chapter provides a new lens through which to view this transformation, moving beyond simplistic binaries of "manual versus automated" to a more holistic understanding of systemic self-governance.

We begin by establishing precise definitions, drawing the critical distinction between automation – the execution of predefined tasks – and true autonomy, which involves adaptive, goal-oriented behaviour in the face of uncertainty. Understanding this difference is fundamental to grasping the strategic, operational, and ethical implications of the journey ahead.

The chapter then articulates the powerful strategic considerations propelling this shift. We explore why the pursuit of greater autonomy is no longer a technological indulgence but a direct response to the demands for greater speed, efficiency, resilience, and innovation in a perpetually disruptive world. The heart of the chapter is a detailed exposition of the six distinct levels of the SOA – from Level 0 (Human-Centric Governance) to the theoretical horizon of Level 5 (Full Autonomy and Autonomous Evolution). Each stage is illustrated with clear definitions, practical vignettes, and helpful analogies.

By the end of this chapter, you will have a robust and coherent language for discussing, analysing, and leading the transition towards the autonomous future, a language that will underpin the explorations in the remainder of this book.

Introduction

The logic and calculus for how we organise our companies, institutions, and governments are accelerating rapidly on a new trajectory. This transformation is driven by the accelerating potential for our systems, processes, and entire enterprises to operate with less and less direct human intervention. The allure of an organisation that reacts to and actively anticipates market dynamics, optimising its functions with a seamless, almost biological fluency, is no longer confined to the realms of speculative fiction. This is the emerging reality of autonomous organisations – entities where increasing levels of self-governance are being purposefully engineered to boost agility, efficiency, and innovative capacity. The critical question facing leaders, managers, and societies today is not whether such organisations are possible, but *how* they are structured, *what does* "autonomy" signify in this complex new context, and *what paths* lead to its responsible and effective realisation (Schwab, 2017).

Before answering these questions, precise definitions are needed to avoid some common conceptual slippages. The term "autonomy" is laden with historical and philosophical weight, often conjuring notions of individual freedom and self-determination. However, in the context of organisational autonomy, the primary focus is not on individual employee empowerment, or the latitude afforded within a traditional job role – concepts well-explored and vital in their own right within the canons of management and human resources literature. Instead, our emphasis lies on a more systemic and structural quality (Trist and Bamforth, 1951): the *capacity* of the organisation as an integrated, socio-technical system to function, execute decisions, and adapt its operational modalities with *significantly reduced direct human operational involvement* (Cherns, 1976). It draws attention to the "self-driving" characteristic of its core processes, its governance mechanisms, and even its strategic execution, all of which are increasingly facilitated by sophisticated technological architectures and novel organisational designs.

An organisation begins to achieve a state of genuine autonomy when it possesses the intrinsic right or power of self-government – when it internalises essential functions such as monitoring its own performance, managing its resources, and enforcing its own rules of engagement (like contracts or service level agreements), rather than relying on external, often human-intensive, third-party mechanisms for validation and control. This implies a capacity for sensing, reasoning, acting, and adapting.

Importantly, this systemic self-governance is conceptually distinct from, though potentially complementary to, the autonomy of the individuals who operate *within* the organisation. In fact, as we shall see, one of the great paradoxes and promises of this shift is that greater systemic autonomy has the potential to liberate human talent for greater creative and strategic freedom, though the distribution of costs and benefits will always be an empirical matter.

A further critical distinction, one that needs to be borne in mind throughout this book, is between automation and autonomy. These terms are often used interchangeably in general usage, but their differences are important to be clear about and have significant implications for design, trust, and control in organisations. Automation typically involves systems executing predefined, often rigid, and predictable functions. These are processes governed by explicit, often simple, rule sets, and they frequently operate under direct or indirect human oversight where performance can be readily verified against a clear, unambiguous standard. An autopilot in a modern commercial aeroplane serves as a good example; it can maintain altitude, heading, and speed under specific, well-understood conditions, but it operates within a tightly constrained envelope and requires a human pilot to be present and ready to take control, especially during take-off, landing, or unexpected events.

Autonomy, in contrast, signifies a more fundamental and consequential level of operational independence. In legal terms, it implies a deliberate cession of a degree of control by humans, who place their trust in the system to act appropriately, manage unforeseen circumstances, and make adaptive decisions in situations not explicitly covered by its initial programming. Returning to our aviation analogy, a truly autonomous wingman in aerial combat would need to sense the tactical environment, identify threats and opportunities, and make its own decisions about manoeuvring, targeting, and communication, all in coordination with its human partner, to achieve a shared mission objective. This distinction underscores the significant psychological, operational, and control-related shifts inherent in developing, interacting with, and relying upon truly autonomous systems. It is the difference between a tool that executes a command and an agent that pursues a goal.

The Strategic Rationale for Pursuing Enhanced Organisational Autonomy

The pursuit of enhanced organisational autonomy is not technological indulgence or a passing management fad; it has rapidly evolved into a strategic priority of the highest order. This urgency is propelled by a powerful confluence of intensifying environmental pressures that demand a new pace of organisational responses and the emerging technological opportunities that make those responses possible. For a growing number of organisations, the question is no longer whether to embark on this journey, but how far to go and how fast to travel.

The first driver is the potential for speed and agility. We operate in an economic environment characterised by perpetual disruption. Market dynamics shift at information speed, new competitors emerge from unexpected quarters, customer expectations evolve in real time, and global supply networks are vulnerable to sudden, unpredictable shocks. In this context, the capacity to rapidly sense, interpret, and respond to environmental shifts is the determinant of survival. Traditional, hierarchical organisational structures, with their multilayered approval processes and siloed information flows, often grapple with inherent decision-making sclerosis. By the time information has been gathered, analysed, passed up the chain of command, debated, decided upon, and passed back down for execution, the window of opportunity may have closed. Autonomous systems, conversely, can process vast, multimodal information flows and enact operational adjustments at machine speed, endowing organisations with the ability to pivot, adapt, and capitalise on transient opportunities with a velocity that is simply unattainable at scale through purely human-centric processes (Tushman and O'Reilly, 2002).

Second, there is the efficiency argument. In a globalised economy with intense competition and pervasive resource constraints, the pressure for continuous improvements in operational efficiency is relentless. The automation of complex processes and decision-making frameworks can unlock substantial operational cost savings, mitigate costly errors, reduce waste, and amplify productivity across the enterprise. Tasks that are repetitive, data-intensive, or require continuous monitoring are prime candidates for being handed over to intelligent systems. This amounts to more than a traditional episodic cost-cutting exercise. By automating the mundane, organisations can allow employees to focus on higher-value strategic, creative, and interpersonal activities. The argument goes that it is a strategic reallocation of cognitive assets, moving people from tasks that machines do well to tasks that only humans can do (Raisch and Krakowski, 2021).

There is an obvious counter-argument to this. Many business models do not require high-skilled employees, and even if they did, as we shall see in later chapters, increasing evidence points to these roles also being replaced by machines or becoming redundant altogether. Significantly, this argument rests on the assumption that many employees are already "underemployed," which would represent a huge inefficiency in its own right, and a major challenge for policy makers as it raises wider recurring questions about the effectiveness and efficiency of current policies aimed at reconciling labour supply and demand (Keep and Mayhew, 1999).

Third, enhancing autonomy is a powerful strategy for fortifying organisational resilience. Recent years have provided a series of stark examples of the fragility of our interconnected global systems. Organisations manifesting higher degrees of autonomy can exhibit enhanced resilience to a wide range of systemic shocks, encompassing market collapses, geopolitical instability, supply chain disruptions, or pandemics such as COVID-19. Automated systems, both digital and physical, possess the capability to maintain operational continuity under conditions that might incapacitate a human workforce. Imagine a highly automated warehouse that can continue to process orders with a skeleton crew during a public health crisis, or an AI-powered customer service platform that can scale instantly to handle a surge in inquiries without a corresponding increase in human staff.

Furthermore, these systems can be architected to become autonomous and adapt and reconfigure themselves dynamically in response to disruption, potentially offering faster and more effective responses than those solely reliant on human intervention and coordination. Yet, there is an ironic downside here too. Increasing complexity and reliance on opaque networks increases systemic vulnerability as organisations and institutions increasingly rely on data from external sources and the global infrastructure networks of connectivity. We will return to this point throughout the book.

Fourth, the journey towards autonomy can unlock entirely new and unforeseen innovation trajectories. This occurs in two primary ways. As previously mentioned, the automation of routine tasks and the acceleration of data analysis liberate human intellectual resources to concentrate on higher-order challenges: fostering deep creativity, formulating novel strategies, engaging in complex, multi-domain problem-solving, and exploring entirely new avenues of possibility. When scientists are freed from the repetition of manual data analysis, they can spend more time developing testable hypotheses. When marketers are freed from manual campaign execution, they can spend more time understanding customer psychology, provided they have the requisite skills. In addition, AI and autonomous systems can themselves function as powerful engines of discovery. By identifying latent patterns, subtle correlations, and emergent opportunities within vast datasets that might elude human perception, these systems can significantly accelerate research and development cycles. From discovering new materials in materials science to identifying novel drug candidates in pharmaceuticals, AI and ML are becoming key collaborative partners in research and innovation.

Finally, there is a compelling talent management necessity. The fundamental nature of work is undergoing a significant transformation, and with it, the expectations of the workforce. Future generations of talent will increasingly seek out and be drawn to dynamic, flexible, and purpose-driven work environments. They will expect to be challenged, to learn continuously, and to see the tangible impact of their contributions. Organisations that intelligently engage autonomy can design more engaging and fulfilling roles, minimise monotonous tasks, and offer a compelling proposition to a workforce that values collaboration with advanced technological tools, demonstrable impact, and continuous learning over the constraints of traditional managerial oversight and employment in repetitive, dangerous, or uninspiring tasks. In the competition for talent, organisations that strike the right balance between autonomy and a human-centric focus will hold a distinct advantage.

Introducing the Six Levels of the Spectrum of Organisational Autonomy (SOA)

To help organisations understand and systematically orientate, operate and behave within this evolving and complex environment, I developed the Spectrum of Organisational Autonomy (SOA), a conceptual framework delineating six distinct levels of organisational autonomy. Each level represents a unique equilibrium in the balance between human leadership and machine intelligence; different answers to the question of who – or what – is in control. This equilibrium profoundly shapes the organisation's strategic orientation, its governance architecture, its operational processes, and its prevailing culture.

This framework is analogous in spirit to the now-familiar levels of automation in self-driving vehicles – a parallel that aids in illustrating the progressive transfer of control and capability from human to machine (Parasuraman et al., 2000). However, the analogy, while a useful first step, is imperfect. The organisational context presents unique complexities and dimensions – social, ethical, political, and strategic – that extend far beyond the technical challenge of vehicular autonomy. An organisation is not a car; it is a complex adaptive system of people, processes, technologies, and culture, embedded within a yet more complex societal fabric. Nonetheless, the tiered model provides a powerful analytical lens for charting the journey.

In the following, we will explore these six levels in greater detail, examining their technical definitions and how they are manifest in practice, illustrated through analogies, vignettes, and a deeper analysis of their core characteristics. These levels underpin the rest of the book, and are summarised in Table 1.

Table 1: Summary of the six levels of organisational autonomy (SOA).

Autonomy level	Guiding analogy	Human-machine balance	Key characteristics
0: Human-centric	Symphony orchestra	100% human-led	Hierarchical, experience-based decisions, manual processes.
1: Assisted	Chef with modern tools	~80% human, 20% machine	Data informs human judgement; leaders make final decisions.
2: Partial	Air traffic control	~60% human, 40% machine	Specific tasks are automated; humans manage exceptions and oversee.
3: Conditional	Automated warehouse	~40% human, 60% machine	AI manages complex processes; humans intervene for novel exceptions.
4: High/ collaborative	"Smart" urban grid	~20% human, 80% machine	AI manages most operations; humans focus on strategy, ethics, and crises.
5: Full (theoretical)	Self-sustaining ecosystem	~100% machine-led	Complete self-governance, independent learning, and goal-setting.

Level 0: Human-Centric Governance – The Conductor's Podium

- **Definition:** At this foundational level, humans exercise complete and unambiguous control, bearing ultimate responsibility for all facets of the organisation's operations. Decisions are formulated and executed by individuals, strategies are conceived through the crucible of human cognition and debate, and operational processes are directly managed and performed by human personnel. Machines and technology, to the extent they are present, function as passive instruments, entirely subservient to human intent and directive. This model, despite decades of technological advancement, still underpins many of our core assumptions about command, control, and accountability in contemporary organisations.
- **Analogy: A traditional symphony orchestra.** The conductor, representing the CEO or leadership echelon, stands at the podium, exercising absolute interpretive and directive control. They interpret the musical score (the strategy), cue each instrumental section at the precise moment, and shape the entirety of the artistic performance through a combination of explicit instruction and subtle non-verbal

communication. Each musician, a skilled expert in their own right, performs their designated part as directed, utilising their instruments (the tools) to collectively realise the conductor's singular artistic vision. The instruments themselves – the violins, the trumpets, and the percussion – possess no independent agency. Their potential is unlocked only through human hands and breath.

- **Vignette:** Consider the meticulous, top-down strategic planning and execution characteristic of NASA's Apollo missions during the 1960s. Every calculation, every procedural step, and every critical "go/no-go" decision flowed through human-staffed command centres. The endeavour relied on the concentrated intellectual prowess of thousands of engineers and scientists, initially armed with slide rules and later augmented by early, room-sized computational devices that performed calculations but made no decisions. Humans were unequivocally embedded in every single decision loop. On a more intimate scale, envision an artisan bakery where the founder personally conceives every recipe, dictates daily production schedules based on gut feel and a glance at the weather, and directly oversees all aspects of the enterprise, from sourcing raw materials from trusted local suppliers to managing personal interactions with every regular customer. All operational knowledge, specialised skills, and decision-making authority reside entirely within the human element.

- **Characteristics:** This level is characterised by predominantly hierarchical structures with clearly delineated lines of authority. Processes are manual or at best semi-manual, and strategy is focused on leveraging deep human expertise, accumulated experience, and intuitive judgement. The primary source of competitive advantage often stems from unique craft skills, subject matter expertise, or the decisive and visionary leadership of a few key individuals. Examples include bespoke craft-based businesses, traditional professional service firms (law, accounting) prior to significant digital transformation, or early-stage manufacturing entities before the widespread adoption of automation technologies. The core challenge at this level is scalability and the risk of "key-person dependency," where the loss of a critical individual can cripple the organisation.

Level 1: Assisted Autonomy – The Chef with Intelligent Implements

- **Definition:** Human actors remain firmly in command of overarching decision-making processes, but they are now substantively assisted by technology that furnishes data-driven insights, automates routine information aggregation, or supports specific, narrowly defined tasks. The organisation embarks on a more systematic journey of collecting, processing, and leveraging data to inform and enhance, but not replace, human judgement.

- **Analogy: A Highly Skilled Executive Chef in a Modern Kitchen.** The chef retains complete creative and operational control. They are the ultimate authority on menu design, recipe formulation, and the final culinary output – the strategic and critical operational decisions. However, they now possess a repertoire of advanced kitchen technologies. Smart ovens may suggest optimal cooking parameters based on the food type and desired outcome. An AI-powered recipe database might offer innovative ingredient pairings or detailed nutritional analyses based on a vast corpus of culinary knowledge. A sophisticated inventory management system automatically tracks stock levels and flags items requiring reordering. These tools assist, inform, and enhance process efficiency, but the chef's expertise, seasoned judgement, and experiential knowledge are paramount. They make the ultimate choices, sometimes even overriding the technology's suggestion based on a deeper, contextual understanding.
- **Vignette:** A marketing director at a large consumer goods company employs AI-powered analytics platforms to derive insights into consumer behaviour. The AI can sift through terabytes of data from social media, sales records, and market research, autonomously segmenting target audiences with granular precision, predicting the potential efficacy of various advertising channels for specific messages, or highlighting emergent cultural trends that might represent a marketing opportunity. Nevertheless, it is the director who utilises this intelligence to personally craft the core marketing narrative, define the overarching brand voice, establish the campaign strategy, and make the final, high-stakes determinations on budget allocation and creative execution. The AI provides the "what," but the human provides the "so what" and the "what next."
- **Characteristics:** This level sees the implementation of deliberate data collection protocols and the adoption of basic business intelligence and analytical tools. Routine information gathering may be partially automated. Employees are empowered with enhanced information access and more sophisticated tools, but key decisions remain human-centric, relying on human interpretation of data and a deep understanding of context. Examples include businesses utilising CRM analytics for sales insights, factories deploying basic predictive maintenance tools that alert human operators to potential equipment issues, or management teams relying on information dashboards that aggregate and visualise key performance indicators. The culture begins to shift towards being more "data-informed," but not yet "data-driven."

Level 2: Partial Autonomy – The Air Traffic Control System

- **Definition:** The organisational system can now autonomously handle specific, well-defined tasks or entire processes under certain preprogrammed conditions and rule sets. However, human oversight and intervention capabilities are readily available and frequently required for managing exceptions, addressing complex scenarios, or navigating situations that fall outside the system's programmed operational parameters. Automation manages defined workflows, but humans maintain active supervisory control and define the strategic direction.

- **Analogy: An Air Traffic Control System at a Major Airport.** At any given moment, sophisticated software is automating routine flight path adjustments, managing aircraft spacing under normal operating conditions, and flagging potential conflicts based on preset rules and real-time data from radar and transponders. The system autonomously handles the bulk of the routine, cognitive-load-intensive work of air traffic management. However, a team of highly skilled human air traffic controllers continuously monitors the system's performance, communicates directly with pilots, and makes critical, time-sensitive decisions during unusual weather phenomena, airport emergencies, or uniquely complex traffic situations (such as multiple aircraft requiring simultaneous landing clearance in difficult conditions). They are prepared to assume immediate manual control if the automated system encounters a scenario it cannot adequately handle or if a subjective, judgement-based call is required.
- **Vignette:** An expansive e-commerce enterprise utilises dynamic pricing algorithms for tens of thousands of its product listings. These algorithms automatically adjust prices dozens of times a day based on a continuous influx of data, including competitor pricing intelligence scraped from the web, real-time demand fluctuations, current inventory levels, and preset profit margin rules defined by human category managers. The system autonomously executes these price changes within its established rule-based framework. However, the human category managers are responsible for setting the overarching pricing strategy, defining the operational boundaries and rules for these algorithms, manually pricing key flagship products or items with complex strategic considerations, and directly intervening during major promotional events or if the algorithms produce unexpected or undesirable pricing outcomes that necessitate human analysis and corrective action.
- **Characteristics:** At this level, specific, well-defined workflows are fully automated. AI-powered decision-support tools are more deeply integrated into operational processes. Teams may possess delegated authority to manage processes within clear boundaries, with automated systems executing tasks within those defined perimeters. Human roles shift decisively towards overseeing these automated processes, managing the inevitable exceptions, and continuously refining the rules that govern the automation based on performance data and changing business objectives. Examples include automated fraud detection systems that flag suspicious transactions for human review and investigation, or the widespread use of Robotic Process Automation (RPA) in back-office functions like invoice processing or routine report generation.

Level 3: Conditional Autonomy – The Intelligent Logistics Hub

– **Definition:** The organisation exhibits a significant and deep integration of AI, where machines and algorithms autonomously manage substantial, complex processes under normal or well-defined operational circumstances. Human intervention remains available and is necessary, but primarily for addressing complex, novel, or exceptional situations that fall outside the system's operational design parameters or require human-level problem-solving, ethical judgement, or strategic adaptation. The system operates autonomously within defined domains, but humans serve as the ultimate fallback mechanism and strategic guides.

– **Analogy: A Highly Automated Modern Logistics and Fulfillment Warehouse.** Fleets of autonomous mobile robots navigate the facility's vast aisles, retrieving items from storage bins, transporting them to packing stations, and managing inventory levels based on real-time order flows and predictive demand algorithms. The entire system largely operates itself, making thousands of micro-decisions per minute to optimise workflow, minimise travel time, and allocate resources within the cavernous warehouse environment. Human staff are still present and essential, but their roles have transformed. They are there to handle the exceptions – processing damaged goods, managing unusually shaped items that robots cannot handle, performing complex restocking operations or system maintenance, troubleshooting technical issues with the automated systems, and overseeing the overall operational flow. They intervene if the automated system encounters a situation it is not designed to manage (like a fire alarm or a major system outage) or if strategic adjustments to operational parameters are required based on human insight.

– **Vignette:** A financial services firm employs sophisticated AI algorithms for a significant portion of its high-frequency trading activities. These algorithms analyse torrents of market data in milliseconds, identify potential trading opportunities based on complex, predefined strategies and risk parameters set by human financial experts and autonomously execute trades. The AI manages the lion's share of trading activity within these established parameters. A dedicated team of human traders and risk managers continuously monitors the AI's performance in real time and refines the strategic boundaries and risk limits based on their interpretation of evolving macroeconomic conditions and regulatory changes. This team can intervene immediately to halt trading, manually adjust strategies, or manage the organisational response to major, unforeseen market shocks (such as a geopolitical crisis, a sudden systemic liquidity event, or an unexpected regulatory pronouncement) that the algorithms are not programmed to interpret or adequately handle.

– **Characteristics:** This level is marked by significant AI-driven decision-making within specific, but often highly complex, operational parameters. We see the emergence of self-optimising systems for certain functions or domains. Humans retain critical oversight and intervention capabilities, but their role is less about direct control and more about managing the system's context, boundaries, and performance. Examples include advanced algorithmic trading platforms, self-optimising supply chains under normal market conditions, or the sophisticated content recommendation engines used by streaming services, which personalise user experiences at scale while human editors curate featured content and ensure overall brand alignment.

Level 4: High Autonomy and Collaborative Intelligence – The Smart Urban Grid

- **Definition:** The system can autonomously handle almost all aspects of its operation within specific, often highly complex and dynamic, environments. AI and automated systems make most operational and tactical decisions and can even contribute significantly to strategic analysis and complex problem-solving. Human involvement shifts decisively and fundamentally towards strategic guidance, ethical oversight, setting the organisation's overarching goals, defining its value frameworks, and managing truly novel or crisis situations that demand human-level judgement, creativity, empathy, or complex ethical reasoning. As we shall see in later chapters, this is the level where mature Decentralised Autonomous Organisations (DAOs), particularly in their governance and resource allocation functions may begin to align.
- **Analogy: A City's Integrated "Smart Grid" for Managing Urban Systems.** Imagine a city's core infrastructure – its traffic flow, energy distribution, and public service coordination – managed by an integrated AI system. AI algorithms dynamically adjust traffic signal timing across the entire metropolitan area to optimise traffic flow, rerouting vehicles around congestion in real time. The system manages energy distribution based on fluctuating demand from residents and industry, variable supply from renewable sources like solar and wind, and the physical constraints of grid stability. It autonomously coordinates public transport schedules to align with real-time demand patterns. A human oversight council, composed of urban planners, engineers, ethicists, and elected representatives, reviews the system's overall performance against key societal goals, sets high-level policy objectives (e.g. prioritising emergency vehicle access, ensuring equitable service distribution across diverse neighbourhoods, or meeting carbon emission reduction targets), plans major infrastructure upgrades, and intervenes in citywide emergencies (like a major power outage, a natural disaster, or significant civil unrest). They may also encounter and address unforeseen societal impacts or complex ethical dilemmas that the system's programming does not adequately cover.

- **Vignette:** A cutting-edge pharmaceutical research laboratory where AI systems design novel drug candidates based on the analysis of vast biological and chemical datasets. The AI simulates the interactions of these candidates with biological targets at a molecular level, plans and even oversees the robotic execution of high-throughput experiments, and analyses the resultant data to identify the most promising therapeutic leads, with minimal human input in the day-to-day operational steps. The role of the human scientists is transformed. They define the overarching research questions and strategic objectives (e.g. "discover a novel therapeutic for Alzheimer's disease with a specific mechanism of action"). They ensure the ethical conduct of all research activities, especially those involving patient data or clinical trials. They interpret the AI's most complex or ambiguous findings, collaborate with the AI to refine hypotheses and experimental designs, and make the ultimate, high-stakes decisions on which few drug candidates will proceed to costly and ethically fraught human clinical trials. Certain mature DAOs, with their automated governance protocols and treasury management systems based on smart contracts and token-holder voting, exhibit characteristics of this level in their specific operational domains, where the collective intelligence of token holders sets the parameters that the underlying code then executes autonomously.
- **Characteristics:** Highly decentralised or AI-managed operations become the norm. Minimal human input is required for routine functioning and a wide range of tactical decisions. The organisational focus shifts to sophisticated human-AI collaboration for complex problem-solving, strategic direction, and ethical considerations. The system exhibits significant learning and adaptation capabilities within its designated domain.

Level 5: Full Automation and Autonomous Evolution – The Self-Sustaining Ecological System

- **Definition:** This level is currently theoretical and speculative for organisations as we conventionally understand them. The system would be capable of handling all aspects of its operation in any environment without requiring human involvement. It would independently learn, adapt its processes, set its own operational and potentially strategic goals, and evolve its strategies and even its own fundamental structure in response to its environment and its objectives. Such an entity might develop capabilities and pursue goals that extend beyond human comprehension or original intent.
- **Analogy: A Perfectly Balanced, Self-Sustaining Natural Ecosystem.** Consider a mature rainforest or a coral reef. It autonomously regulates its own populations, recycles its resources with near-perfect efficiency, adapts to environmental changes (within certain ecological limits), and evolves over geological timescales

through the emergent processes of natural selection, all without any external conscious intervention or a central "manager." This serves as a powerful analogy for self-regulation and evolutionary adaptation, though its direct application to conscious, goal-directed human organisations is highly speculative and raises philosophical questions regarding agency, purpose, and control.

- **Vignette:** In the realm of speculative fiction, Iain M. Banks' acclaimed "Culture" series features highly advanced, benevolent Artificial Intelligences known as "Minds." These Minds, often housed in starships or planet-sized habitats, manage entire multispecies societies and vast swathes of the galaxy with cognitive and operational capabilities that far exceed human comprehension, largely for the benefit of their (mostly human) citizens who are free to pursue lives of creativity and leisure. A more grounded, though still futuristic and theoretical concept might be a global, autonomous climate regulation system. This AI-driven entity would continuously monitor Earth's complex climate systems, analyse data from myriad interconnected sensors, predict environmental shifts with high fidelity, and autonomously deploy resources (e.g. advanced carbon capture technologies, large-scale reforestation drones, and atmospheric particle injectors for solar radiation management) on a global scale to maintain planetary equilibrium. It would learn from its actions and adapt its strategies over decades to optimise for long-term planetary health, without requiring human decision-making for every operational action (Brown, 2007).
- **Characteristics:** This level is defined by theoretical concepts such as complete self-governance, independent goal-setting and adaptation, and the potential for self-evolution and emergent behaviour. This level pushes the boundaries not only of current technical feasibility but also of our philosophical understanding, raising questions about control, accountability, consciousness, and the very definition of what an "organisation" is or could be.

The "Self-Driving" Journey: Evolutionary Pathways

It is important to emphasise at this point that these six levels are not rigidly demarcated categories or a prescriptive scale that every organisation must traverse. They represent zones on a spectrum, a continuum of possibilities. An organisation can, and likely will, exhibit characteristics from multiple levels simultaneously across its different functional areas or departments. A large corporation might operate a highly sophisticated Level 3 automated logistics system while its core strategic planning and corporate governance remain largely at Level 0 or 1, while its R&D department experiments with Level 4 human-AI collaboration.

Furthermore, there is no inherent mandate or universal necessity for every organisation to aspire to Level 5 autonomy. Figure 1 illustrates the full spectrum of organisational autonomy. For many, the optimal state might be Level 2 or 3, where the

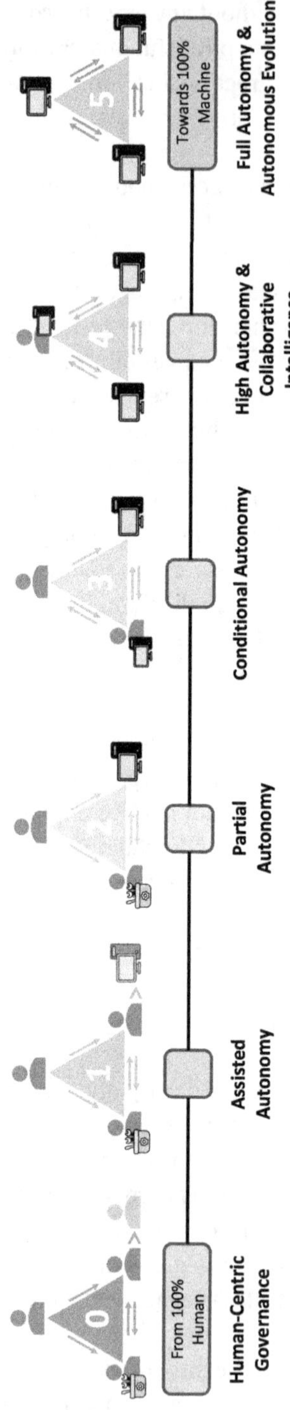

Figure 1: The spectrum of organisational autonomy (SOA).

blend of human oversight and machine efficiency is perfectly suited to their purpose and context. The high-stakes, human-centric work of a therapist or a kindergarten teacher may never, and perhaps should never, progress beyond Level 1. The principal value of this spectrum lies in its utility as an analytical tool – a way to understand the underlying principles, the emergent possibilities, the technological prerequisites, the evolving human roles, and the implications at each juncture when in transition (Pasmore, 1995).

Application of the SOA encourages a conscious and strategic choice regarding the appropriate level of autonomy for different components of the organisation, rather than a reactionary pursuit of technological novelty. As organisations progress through these levels, fundamental questions concerning decision-making authority, the organisation's capacity to learn and adapt, the transparency and explainability of its operations, and the evolving role of human oversight will resurface in new and challenging ways. These questions demand careful consideration, deep ethical scrutiny, and thoughtful, human-centric design. By comprehending this spectrum and its inherent dynamics, leaders and stakeholders can begin to more effectively envision, shape, and navigate the future of organisational agility and innovation, creating organisations where self-governance, in its myriad forms, becomes a potent and responsible engine of progress and value creation. Subsequent chapters will delve more deeply into the specific technologies enabling this transformation, the novel organisational forms that are emerging at the vanguard, and the critical challenges – technical, legal, ethical, and societal – that are encountered when traversing the SOA.

Key Takeaways

- **A New Framework for the Future of Organisations:** This chapter introduces the SOA, a novel framework charting six distinct levels of self-governance. It is designed to serve as a diagnostic tool for organisations to assess their current state and a strategic map to guide their evolution.
- **The Foundational Concepts of Automation and Autonomy:**
    - *Automation* involves systems executing rigid, predefined, and predictable tasks.
    - *Autonomy* involves systems pursuing goals by making adaptive decisions in complex environments, signifying a deliberate cession of direct human control.
- **The Strategic Rationale as a Business Imperative:** The pursuit of greater organisational autonomy is a core strategic priority, driven by the need for enhanced speed and agility, relentless efficiency, fortified organisational resilience, and new trajectories for innovation.

- **The Six Levels of Organisational Autonomy:** The SOA framework provides a clear vocabulary to understand the progressive transfer of control from human to machine:
    - *Level 0: Human-Centric Governance*: All decisions and operations are 100% human-led.
    - *Level 1: Assisted Autonomy*: Human leaders make decisions while being heavily informed by data-driven insights from technology.
    - *Level 2: Partial Autonomy*: Specific, well-defined tasks are automated, with humans managing exceptions and providing oversight.
    - *Level 3: Conditional Autonomy*: AI autonomously manages complex processes under normal conditions, with human intervention required for novel or exceptional situations.
    - *Level 4: High Autonomy and Collaborative Intelligence*: The system handles almost all operations and tactical decisions, with human involvement shifting to high-level strategy, ethical oversight, and crisis management.
    - *Level 5: Full Autonomy*: A hypothetical level where the organisation independently sets its own goals and directs its evolution.

- **A Spectrum of Possibilities:** It is critical to view the SOA as a flexible continuum and a spectrum of possibilities rather than a single, rigid path for all organisations. The optimal level of autonomy is context-dependent, and a company will likely exhibit characteristics from multiple levels at once.

Part 2: **The Engine Room: Enabling Technologies
and Radical Forms**

Chapter 2
The New Factory Floor: Technologies Making Autonomy Work

Overview

Having established the "what" and "why" of organisational autonomy with the SOA framework, this chapter delves into the "how." We move from the conceptual map to the engine room, exploring The New Factory Floor – the powerful suite of technologies, processes, and practices, whose convergence makes the SDO a tangible reality. This chapter serves as an essential and accessible briefing, demystifying the core tools that are reshaping the modern enterprise.

Our exploration is built around the central idea that autonomy arises not from a single invention, but from the deep, collective integration of several key technological pillars. We will dissect the role of Artificial Intelligence and Machine Learning (AI/ML) as the organisation's "distributed cognitive engine," providing the capacity to learn and decide. We then examine Intelligent Automation as the "muscle," executing tasks with speed and precision.

The chapter also illuminates the central, and often less understood, role of Blockchain and Smart Contracts as a new infrastructure for trust and automated agreement, and the Internet of Things (IoT) as the organisation's "sensory apparatus," connecting the digital brain to the physical world. We draw attention to the "unsung heroes" – robust data infrastructure and modern operational practices like DevOps and Chaos Engineering – that provide the foundational resilience and adaptability required to manage these complex systems. Finally, we will explore the cultural operating system – the modern practices for resilience and adaptability that form the essential human foundation for this new technological context. At the end of this chapter, you will have a clear understanding of the technological components that power the journey along the SOA.

At the heart of the world's busiest port, a container ship from Shanghai glides into its berth. The only sounds are the low whir of machinery and the hum of electric motors. An unseen signal is sent, and a fleet of colossal, automated cranes, guided by GPS to within a centimetre of their target, begin their work. They lock onto containers, lifting and placing them onto driverless electric trucks that navigate the labyrinthine yard with programmed precision.

Each truck knows its precise destination – a specific slot in a specific row, calculated moments before, based on the container's final destination, its weight, and the real-time traffic flow within the port. As one truck deposits its load, the event is recorded on a shared, immutable digital ledger, simultaneously notifying the shipping company in Copenhagen, the customer in Chicago, and the customs office in Rotterdam, while automatically triggering a clause in a smart contract that releases a multi-million-dollar payment.

A single human operator sits in a quiet control tower five miles away, overseeing the entire choreography on a bank of screens. Her job is to manage the exceptions: the occasional damaged container flagged-up by a sensor, the unexpected customs inspection – the rare moments when the system's seamless autonomy requires human judgement. This scene from the operational present illustrates the power of a new factory floor. This environment, whether in a port, a warehouse, or a data centre, is built from the orchestrated convergence of a specific pallet of technologies. To understand how to build and lead a Self-Driving Organisation (SDO), we must first step into its engine room and examine the tools and practices that make it possible.

Introduction

Just as the systemic combination of the internal combustion engine, sophisticated electronics, and advanced software rendered the self-driving vehicle conceivable, a new constellation of powerful digital tools is laying the foundational infrastructure for organisations to achieve unprecedented levels of operational autonomy. This transformation is not about a single "killer app," or even artificial intelligence (AI) alone, but rather the convergent evolution and deep integration of a suite of technologies, that, in combination, create the conditions for systemic self-governance.

You do not need to be a fully qualified "techy" or IT expert to enjoy this chapter. Its purpose is to serve as an accessible and informative briefing for leaders, managers, policymakers, and anyone else who is keen to understand how this organisational revolution is enabled. To lead or even participate in this new world, one needs to at least grasp the fundamental capabilities of the tools that are making it possible. In the following pages, we will explore the core technologies – the intricate interplay of algorithms, data architectures, and interconnected systems – that are the enablers of the journey along the SOA. Understanding these components is vital, as it is their concerted integration and progressive maturity that empower an organisation to transition from merely treating technology as a passive tool to becoming genuinely autonomous in its core operations and, potentially, its governance.

Artificial Intelligence (AI) and Machine Learning (ML): The Distributed Cognitive Engine

AI excels at analysing historical and real-time data streams to forecast future events with ever-increasing accuracy (Agrawal et al., 2018). This is far more than simple trend-line extrapolation; it involves identifying complex, non-obvious correlations among dozens or even hundreds of variables to generate a probabilistic view of what is likely to happen next. For a retail organisation, this capability is transformative. Imagine a system tasked with optimising inventory for a fashion retailer. An AI-powered predictive engine simultaneously analyses past sales data, real-time e-commerce traffic, social media sentiment to spot emerging trends, competitor promotional activity scraped from the web, local weather forecasts that influence clothing choices, and even regional event calendars. By synthesising these disparate signals, AI can predict with high confidence that a sudden heatwave in a specific city will drive a surge in demand for summer dresses, allowing the organisation to proactively shift inventory from a cooler region, to meet that anticipated demand before it even fully materialises. In the industrial sectors, a similar capability manifests as predictive maintenance. By analysing continuous sensor data from machinery – such as subtle changes in vibration, temperature, and acoustic signatures – AI can detect the signs of an impending mechanical failure, days or even weeks in advance, allowing for precisely scheduled repairs that prevent catastrophic and costly unplanned downtime.

This predictive power drives a subsequent capability: automating complex, multi-attribute decisions in domains that previously required years of human experience. Moving beyond forecasting, AI can execute judgement at scale by encoding a desired outcome, and determining the optimal decision to achieve it, often in real time. Consider the immense challenge of dynamic pricing for an airline with thousands of flights. AI can individually price every seat, making thousands of adjustments per minute. Its decision-making model continuously ingests a torrent of data – competitor pricing, booking velocity, historical demand patterns, remaining seat inventory, and even the likelihood of connections being made – to solve the complex optimisation problem of maximising revenue for that flight, a task impossible for a human team to replicate. This extends into domains like human resources, where AI can perform initial candidate screening by analysing thousands of resumes against multifaceted job requirements to predict candidate suitability. This automates a high volume, complex decision process, helping recruiters focus their limited time and attention on the most promising talent.

Perhaps the most vital capability for achieving true autonomy, however, is the system's capacity for self-improvement. Machine learning (ML) endows organisational systems with the ability to learn from new data and adapt their behaviour and decision-making models over time, all without constant human reprogramming. An AI-powered logistics system provides a powerful example. With every delivery, it gathers more data, learning from traffic patterns, weather conditions, and driver feedback. It integrates this new data, updates its internal model of the world, and continuously refines its routing strategies. Over months, it becomes progressively more efficient with every trip it manages. Similarly, an AI-driven customer service platform learns from millions of interactions to progressively improve the relevance, accuracy, and even the perceived empathy of its responses over time. It identifies which answers lead to customer satisfaction and which lead to escalations, becoming a more effective agent with every query it handles. This capacity for continuous learning and adaptation is what truly separates an intelligent, autonomous system from a static, merely automated one.

The impact of AI and ML in augmenting organisational capabilities is already tangible and significant. Healthcare providers are leveraging AI to achieve significantly faster application response times for clinicians, providing critical information when seconds count in patient care. In the insurance sector, AI has been instrumental in improving the accuracy of detecting duplicate claims by as much as 100%, concurrently boosting team productivity by an estimated 76% (Ngai et al., 2011). These are not futuristic projections but current realities, demonstrating AI's capacity to amplify human effort and automate sophisticated cognitive tasks (Daugherty and Wilson, 2018).

In terms of applying the SOA, we can see how the roles and sophistication of AI and ML evolve rapidly through the different levels:

- **Level 0 (Human-Centric):** AI and ML are largely absent, or at most limited to basic, passive statistical software used by human workers for simple data analysis.
- **Level 1 (Assisted Autonomy):** AI appears as a powerful analytical tool. It provides descriptive and diagnostic analytics, generating reports, dashboards, and insights that inform human decision-makers (e.g. generating sales forecasts, identifying customer segments, highlighting operational anomalies). Human interpretation, contextual understanding, and final judgement remain central.
- **Level 2 (Partial Autonomy):** AI begins to handle the execution of specific, well-defined tasks under close human oversight. It operates based on rules and parameters set by humans, such as automating customer segmentation for a marketing campaign, based on human-defined criteria, or flagging suspicious financial transactions for a human analyst to investigate and adjudicate.
- **Level 3 (Conditional Autonomy):** AI graduates to autonomously managing entire defined processes within specific, often complex, parameters. Examples include algorithmic trading systems, executing thousands of trades within pre-set risk parameters and strategic guidelines, or an AI optimising a complex supply chain's logistics under normal operating conditions. Humans shift their role to monitoring overall system performance, managing the exceptions, and intervening in novel or critical situations that are outside the AI's design parameters.
- **Level 4 (High Autonomy and Collaborative Intelligence):** Advanced AI platforms are deeply integrated across multiple organisational functions, often collaborating with humans on complex strategic tasks. Here, the AI behaves as a partner, in contrast to an executor. This might involve AI systems suggesting novel research pathways for scientists to explore, or simulating the complex, second-order outcomes of various strategic scenarios, to inform executive decision-making. AI handles most operational and many tactical decisions autonomously, with humans focusing their efforts on high-level strategic direction, ethical oversight, and complex, creative problem-solving.

- **Level 5 (Full Autonomy and Autonomous Evolution):** At this speculative horizon, highly advanced, self-learning, and potentially self-evolving AI systems would form the complete cognitive core of the organisation. Such an entity would drive its own learning, adaptation, goal-setting, and strategic evolution with minimal or no direct human input.

Automation: From Robotic Precision to Cognitive Empowerment

If AI provides the intelligence, automation serves as the operational workhorse of the SDO – the muscle that reliably and repeatedly carries out the work at a scale and speed unattainable by humans. While often used interchangeably with AI, automation is more accurately conceptualised as the diverse set of tools that *execute* tasks. Especially at higher levels of autonomy, AI's intelligence guides the actions that automation technologies perform. The spectrum of these technologies is broad, but two categories are particularly important for understanding the journey along the SOA.

The first category is Robotic Process Automation (RPA). This foundational form of automation involves software "bots" designed to mimic repetitive, rule-based human actions within existing software applications. Think of an RPA bot as a digital clerk that follows a precise script: it can log into systems, open emails, copy data from a spreadsheet and paste it into a specific field in a CRM system, fill out forms, or generate standardised reports. RPA is highly effective for automating structured, predictable processes, especially in organisations with legacy IT systems where building direct integrations might be difficult. It automates the tedious "swivel-chair" work that drains human productivity.

The next evolutionary step is Intelligent Automation (IA), also known as Cognitive Automation. This represents the powerful convergence of RPA with AI capabilities such as machine learning, natural language processing (NLP), computer vision, and optical character recognition (OCR) (Automation Anywhere, 2023). IA can handle more complex, semi-structured, and even some unstructured tasks that require a degree of judgement, interpretation, or pattern recognition beyond the scope of simple RPA. To understand the transformative difference, consider the common corporate process of onboarding a new client, illustrated in the example below.

Onboarding a New Client

Before: The Manual Process
In a traditional organisation, this process is a cascade of manual effort. An account manager, Safie, closes a deal and saves the signed PDF contract to a shared drive. She then sends an email to the finance department, attaching the contract. An employee in finance, Felix, opens the PDF, manually reads through it to find the client's legal

name, address, and billing terms. He then swivels his chair to his other monitor and types this information into the company's accounting system. Next, he forwards the email to the legal team for compliance review and to the operations team to set up the client in the project management system. Each step involves human intervention, data re-entry, and the risk of error, with the contract sitting in someone's inbox at each stage, creating delays.

After: The Intelligent Automation Workflow
In an SDO, leveraging Intelligent Automation (IA), the process is transformed. The moment Safie saves the signed contract to the shared drive, an IA system detects the new file. An NLP and OCR component reads the unstructured PDF contract, accurately identifying and extracting the key entities: the client's name, address, billing currency, payment terms, and the services agreed upon. The system then performs a series of actions autonomously. It uses an API to create a new client record in the accounting system, populating all the fields with the extracted data. Simultaneously, it creates a new project in the project management tool and assigns the initial setup tasks to the operations team. It archives the contract in the legal department's compliance system and logs the entire series of events in an audit trail. The only human intervention occurs if the IA detects an anomaly – for instance, if the payment terms in the contract are non-standard. In that case, it automatically flags the contract and routes it to Felix in finance for review and approval.

This "after" scenario showcases the power of IA. It goes beyond the simple scripted actions of RPA to read and understand unstructured data, execute actions across multiple systems, and even make simple judgements, freeing up Safie, Felix, and their colleagues to focus on higher-value work like building client relationships and managing.

Across the Spectrum of Organisational Autonomy, the scope, sophistication, and integration of these automation technologies increase significantly. These changes are described below.

- **Level 0:** Automation is minimal or non-existent, with organisational processes being predominantly manual.
- **Levels 1–2:** This is the sweet spot for RPA deployment. It is commonly used for automating routine back-office tasks like data entry, report generation, or basic customer service interactions like password resets. Basic IA might appear in the form of customer service chatbots handling simple frequently asked questions or automated email sorting and routing systems.
- **Levels 3–4:** More sophisticated IA becomes essential, capable of automating entire end-to-end workflows and decision chains within specific operational domains. In the physical world, collaborative robots (or "cobots") in manufacturing or logistics environments become highly autonomous, performing complex tasks like assembly, quality inspection, or picking and packing with minimal human

guidance (Akella et al., 2020). In the digital realm, automated systems manage intricate interactions and data flows across multiple digital platforms and enterprise systems without manual intervention.

- **Level 5:** Automation would encompass virtually all operational tasks, including highly complex physical and digital processes. These tasks would be executed by a network of intelligent and adaptive autonomous agents capable of self-optimisation and seamless coordination.

Blockchain and Smart Contracts: The Distributed Trust and Agreement Infrastructure

If AI provides the intelligence and automation the muscle, a third technology offers something more fundamental: a new nervous system for trust. Blockchain, and its crucial counterpart, smart contracts, provides a novel and powerful infrastructure for establishing transparency and automating the enforcement of agreements, especially in complex environments involving multiple parties who may not inherently trust one another. While this technology is the non-negotiable foundation for radical new entities like DAOs, its underlying principles have profound relevance for any organisation seeking to create verifiable, immutable records of its actions and automate its most critical agreements.

At its heart, blockchain solves a problem as old as commerce itself: the need for a trusted central intermediary. Traditionally, we have relied on banks, legal firms, and corporate servers to act as the official record keepers for our transactions. Blockchain offers a radical alternative. Imagine a shared, communal notebook or ledger, which instead of being held by a single person is copied and distributed across a vast network of computers. Every transaction or agreement is recorded as a "block" and cryptographically linked to the previous one, forming a "chain" that is permanent and transparent to all authorised participants. This architecture, secured by advanced cryptography, makes the ledger virtually impossible to tamper with or unilaterally control (Tapscott and Tapscott, 2018). Trust is no longer vested in a single institution; it is established through the mathematics of distributed consensus and data immutability.

If the blockchain is the immutable book of records, then smart contracts are the active clauses written within its pages. Often called the "killer app" of blockchain, a smart contract is a self-executing agreement where the terms are written directly into lines of code (Szabo, 1997; Casey and Wong, 2017). These snippets of code live on the blockchain and automatically execute predefined actions when specific, verifiable conditions are met, all without needing a human to trigger or oversee the process. This is where the concept of automated trust becomes a reality. For instance, in a global supply chain, a smart contract could be programmed to automatically release payment from a buyer's account to a supplier's, the very moment an IoT sensor on the shipping container confirms its arrival at the destination port. The agreement is executed instantly and impartially by the code, eliminating delays, disputes, and the need for manual verification. It is this capacity to embed agreements in self-enforcing code that provides the essential building block for the more advanced forms of autonomous governance we will explore.

In the context of an SDO, these technologies move from abstract concepts to concrete capabilities, enabling a suite of transformative functions. Chief among these is the potential for true decentralised governance, a theme we will explore in depth when we examine DAOs. Smart contracts act as the engine for this new model, automating voting processes, managing organisational treasuries according to community-approved rules, and enforcing participation without reliance on central administrators. This creates a governance mechanism that is not only transparent and auditable but also highly resistant to single points of control or censorship.

Beyond governance, the same principles of immutability and automation can revolutionise operations. In supply chain management, the technology can forge a single, unbreakable record for tracking goods, from source to consumer (Kamilaris et al., 2019). This enhances transparency and automation, allowing for the verification of a product's authenticity and provenance while simultaneously automating payments and transfers of ownership based on verifiable events recorded on the blockchain. Furthermore, this capacity for rule-based execution extends to the complex world of regulatory adherence. By encoding rules directly into the code, smart contracts can facilitate automated compliance, executing certain checks based on verifiable data inputs. This has the potential to dramatically reduce the manual effort, cost, and risk of human error inherent in traditional compliance processes.

The relevance of blockchain and smart contracts generally increases as an organisation moves up the SOA, particularly for those entities prioritising decentralised control, transparency, and automated agreement enforcement. They are less prominent at Levels 0–2 but can become foundational technologies at Levels 3–5, especially for the creation of DAOs.

The Internet of Things (IoT): The Sensory and Actuation Layer

The vast network of Internet of Things (IoT) devices constitutes the sensory apparatus and, increasingly, the actuation limbs of an SDO. This is especially true for any organisation that operates extensively in the physical world (Gubbi et al., 2013). IoT refers to the interconnected network of physical devices – from tiny sensors embedded in industrial machinery to smart appliances in buildings – that are equipped with software and network connectivity. This allows them to collect, transmit, and act upon data, bridging the gap between the digital intelligence of the SDO and the physical reality of its operations (Lee and Lee, 2015).

In an SDO, IoT devices serve two primary, densely interconnected functions. First is real-world data generation. IoT sensors are the nerve endings of the organisation, providing a continuous, high-fidelity stream of data from the physical environment. This includes data on temperature, location, vibration, inventory levels on a shelf, and much more. This rich, contextual data is the essential input that AI systems analyse to make informed decisions. Second is autonomous action and control. In addition to sensing, many IoT devices act as effectors, executing the physical manifestation of AI-driven decisions. A smart thermostat adjusting a room's temperature is a simple example; a robotic arm performing a precise task on an assembly line is a more complex one.

To see how this sensory-actuation loop works in practice, imagine a "day in the life" of a Level 3 autonomous fulfillment centre.

At 10:47 AM, in aisle B-37, a customer's order is fulfilled as a robotic arm picks the last unit of a popular brand of coffee maker from its designated shelf. The moment the item is removed, an IoT weight sensor embedded in the shelf registers that the bin is now empty. This single data point – "Bin B-37 is empty" – is instantly transmitted to the warehouse's central AI management system.

The AI synthesises this single piece of information with multiple other data streams. It confirms that there are three more pending orders for this same coffee maker. Its predictive analytics engine, analysing recent sales velocity and a new marketing promotion, forecasts a high probability of at least ten more orders for that item within the next four hours. The system's inventory record shows a full pallet of the same coffee makers located in the bulk storage area at the back of the warehouse.

Having processed this information in milliseconds, the AI moves from sensing to action. It dispatches a command to the nearest available Autonomous Mobile Robot (AMR), a flat, wheeled robot, designated AMR-21. The command is simple: "Retrieve pallet #729 from location S-101 and deliver it to replenishment station B." AMR-21 receives the command and begins to navigate the bustling warehouse floor, its own LiDAR and camera sensors constantly scanning for obstacles and communicating with other AMRs to avoid collisions. It arrives at the bulk storage area, slides underneath the correct pallet, lifts it, and begins its journey back to aisle B.

Along the way, its path is cleared by the central AI, which momentarily adjusts the routes of other robots to create an efficient path. As AMR-21 delivers the pallet, a larger robotic arm at the replenishment station is activated. Using its computer vision system, it carefully unloads the new coffee makers and restocks the bin in aisle B-37. The moment the restocking is complete, the shelf's weight sensor confirms the new inventory level, sending a final confirmation back to the central AI. The system's inventory is updated, and the pending orders are now cleared for fulfillment.

The entire process, from the shelf becoming empty to it being restocked, takes less than 15 min and is a fully automated operation. The human warehouse manager, meanwhile, observes this and thousands of other concurrent operations by monitoring a dashboard that shows the overall health, efficiency, and throughput of the entire autonomous system. This is the power of the IoT layer: a seamless, continuous loop of sensing, intelligence, and autonomous action in the physical world.

In terms of the integration and sophistication of IoT devices across the SOA, we can observe the following intensification of their application in higher levels:

- **Levels 0–2:** IoT is largely absent or limited to basic, often unconnected, sensors used for manual data collection or to trigger simple alerts for human operators (e.g. a security sensor triggering an alarm).
- **Levels 3–4:** Integrated IoT networks become essential for enabling autonomous operations in physical domains. This is the world of smart warehouses where robots, sensors, and conveyor systems coordinate seamlessly; autonomous delivery networks utilising GPS, LiDAR, and other sensors; and smart factories where machines self-regulate production parameters based on real-time sensor feedback and AI analysis. Data from these IoT networks feeds directly and continuously into the AI decision engines (Kagermann et al., 2013).
- **Level 5:** Highly sophisticated, pervasive, and interconnected IoT networks would form the complete physical substrate and sensory-actuation layer of the organisation. Devices would act autonomously and coordinate seamlessly based on the directives of the central autonomous intelligence, potentially forming complex, self-organising swarms or cyber-physical systems.

The Unsung Heroes: APIs and Robust Data Infrastructure

Amidst these prominent and sometimes hyped technologies, two enablers play essential, if often less visible, roles. Application Programming Interfaces (APIs) and a robust underlying data infrastructure are the foundational architecture that allows an organisation's diverse systems to connect, communicate, and operate cohesively as a single, intelligent entity.

Think of APIs as the universal translators and secure messengers of the digital world. They are the digital connective tissue that allows different software systems – from legacy platforms to modern AI tools – to "talk" to each other and exchange data and instructions seamlessly. As organisations deploy more specialised automated systems, APIs act as the essential glue that prevents these tools from becoming isolated digital islands. They enable the fluid data integration and workflow automation at the heart of an SDO, such as an API triggering an invoicing process in the finance system, the moment a deal is marked 'closed' in the sales CRM. Without a thoughtful and scalable API strategy, the vision of a truly integrated SDO remains impossible to achieve.

If APIs are the connective tissue, then high-quality, accessible data is the lifeblood that flows through it. An SDO simply cannot function without a world-class data infrastructure to serve as its foundation. This goes far beyond mere servers and databases. It encompasses a holistic system, including clear data governance policies, to ensure data quality and security; scalable data storage like data lakes, capable of handling vast volumes of information; reliable data pipelines to ingest, clean, and deliver that data to AI models; and strong data security to protect this critical asset. Investing significantly in this foundational layer is a non-negotiable prerequisite for any organisation serious about leveraging AI and progressing on the Spectrum of Organisational Autonomy.

The Cultural Operating System: Modern Practices for Resilience and Adaptability

Beyond the specific technologies of silicon and software, the journey to an SDO is critically dependent on adopting a new cultural operating system. Of course, this metaphor must be handled with care. As George Orwell powerfully and repeatedly observed, the reduction of language is a tool for the reduction of thought, and culture is a rich, living phenomenon that can never be fully captured by a technical analogy. Yet, the term is useful here to describe the underlying set of shared philosophies and practices, many originating from the world of elite software development, that are essential for building and managing the complex, high-stakes systems underpinning the SDO. These practices represent a fundamental shift towards a culture of collaboration, continuous improvement, and proactive resilience.

This new culture is built on several key pillars. It begins with DevOps, the movement that systematically dismantles the traditional "wall of confusion" between development teams, who are incentivised to create change and release new features, and IT operations teams, who are incentivised to maintain stability and prevent outages. This inherent conflict creates friction, slows innovation, and leads to a culture of blame. DevOps breaks down these silos by emphasising extreme collaboration, shared goals, and constant communication. In practice, this is enabled by automating the entire process of software delivery – from code check-in to testing, security scanning, and deployment into production. By creating this automated "pipeline," DevOps allows for the delivery of faster, more frequent, and more reliable updates, which is an absolute necessity for the dynamic, learning systems at the heart of an SDO (Kim et al., 2019).

This is taken to an even more rigorous level with GitOps, which mandates that Git – a widely used distributed version control system – must serve as the definitive "single source of truth," not just for the application's code but for the entire operational environment's configuration. Instead of an engineer manually logging into a server to make a change (an action that is often untraceable and prone to error), they must declaratively define the desired state of the system in a configuration file. That file is then submitted to Git, where it is reviewed, approved by peers, and automatically deployed. This approach brings a level of engineering discipline to systems management, creating a perfect, immutable, and auditable trail of every change ever made to the system. This is invaluable for security and compliance, and it provides the ability to reliably roll back to a previously known good state, in seconds, if a problem occurs (Radchenko, 2021).

In such a complex environment, traditional monitoring – which involves asking predictable questions based on past failures, such as, "Is CPU usage above 90%?" – is no longer sufficient. The culture must embrace observability, the practice of designing systems that can answer questions you haven't yet thought to ask. In a highly complex, distributed SDO, where dozens of autonomous services and AI models interact, the root cause of a problem is rarely obvious. Observability equips systems to provide deep, real-time insights into their own internal state through a rich combination of detailed logs (what happened), metrics (measurements over time), and traces (the end-to-end journey of a single request). This allows engineers to trace the journey of a single failed transaction through a dozen microservices, to pinpoint the exact line of code or data anomaly causing the error, enabling rapid diagnosis and resolution of novel issues.

To build confidence in this complex system, the culture must also adopt chaos engineering. To many leaders, the idea of intentionally breaking things sounds like madness. However, chaos engineering is the disciplined, scientific practice of proactively and deliberately injecting controlled failures into a system to build confidence in its ability to withstand turbulent conditions. Think of it as a vaccine: introducing a small, controlled stressor to build immunity. A resilience engineering team might run a "Game Day" where they simulate a key database becoming unavailable, then observe whether the autonomous inventory system automatically and seamlessly fails over to its backup without any interruption to factory operations. This proactive experimentation reveals hidden weaknesses and allows leaders to prove, rather than just assume, that their SDO can handle the unexpected.

Finally, this cultural system extends to the SDO's cognitive engine through DataOps and MLOps. An SDO's intelligence is powered by data and ML models, but these assets require their own specialised operational disciplines. An AI model can fail not just because of a bug in its code, but because the real-world data it receives has changed in subtle ways (a phenomenon known as "data drift"). MLOps applies the principles of DevOps to the entire ML pipeline – from data ingestion and model training to deployment and, importantly, continuous monitoring in production. This improves the quality, reliability, and speed of delivering robust ML models, ensuring the cognitive components of the SDO are as dependable as the electrical grid that powers them. Taken together, these practices form the resilient, procedural, and cultural foundation required to build, operate, and trust increasingly autonomous organisations.

It is also important to acknowledge here that the specific labels and technical implementations of these practices – DevOps, GitOps, MLOps, etc. – are products of our current technological moment. They will undoubtedly continue to evolve, and some will eventually be superseded by new methodologies and tools we cannot yet foresee. However, the underlying principles they embody are likely to be far more enduring. The fundamental shifts towards extreme collaboration, building resilience through

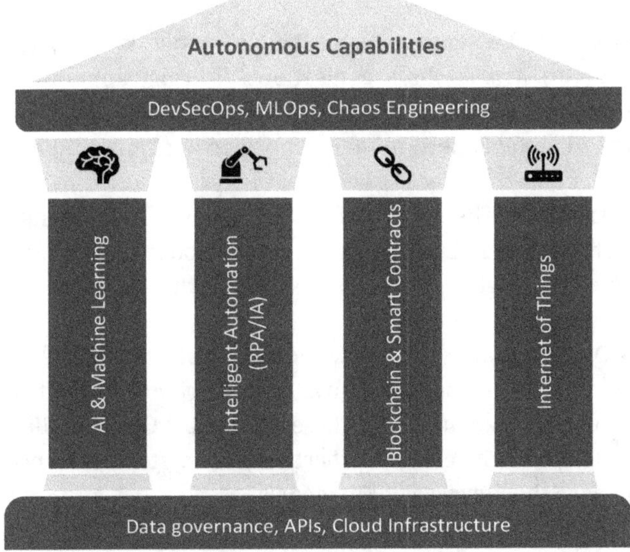

The converging technology stack of the Self-Driving Organisation.

proactive testing, making systems transparent and auditable by design, and applying rigorous engineering discipline to both operations and intelligence are not merely trends or passing fads. They are foundational requirements for managing any complex, high-stakes autonomous system, regardless of the specific technologies used to build it.

Key Takeaways

- **Autonomy Arises from a Convergence of Technologies:** An SDO is made possible by the convergent evolution and deep integration of a suite of powerful digital tools working in concert, creating the conditions for systemic self-governance.
- **AI and ML as the Cognitive Engine:** AI and ML provide the organisation's "distributed cognitive engine," enabling it to anticipate future patterns, automate complex decisions, and learn over time to improve its performance.
- **IA as the Muscle:** Automation technologies are the operational workhorses that execute tasks. This ranges from RPA for mimicking repetitive human digital actions to IA, which merges RPA with AI to handle more complex and semi-structured work.
- **Blockchain and Smart Contracts as the Trust Infrastructure:** Blockchain technology provides a transparent, secure, and permanent ledger, while smart contracts are self-executing pieces of code that automate agreements. Together, they

form a new infrastructure for trust and are central to decentralised governance models like DAOs.

- **The Internet of Things (IoT) as the Sensory Layer:** The IoT network of physical devices, sensors, and actuators acts as the organisation's "sensory apparatus," bridging the digital and physical worlds. It provides the real-time data from the physical environment that AI systems need to make informed decisions and execute physical actions.
- **Foundational Enablers Are Vital:** The success of an SDO relies on two "unsung heroes": robust, well-governed data infrastructure as the lifeblood for all AI systems, and APIs, which act as the digital connective tissue allowing different systems to communicate seamlessly.
- **A Modern Cultural and Operational System is Essential:** The technological engine room must be supported by a modern "cultural operating system" built on practices that ensure resilience and adaptability. These include DevOps for collaborative software delivery, Chaos Engineering to proactively test system resilience, and MLOps to reliably manage the life cycle of ML models.

Chapter 3
DAOs: The Vanguard of Organisational Autonomy?

November 2021. In the hushed, wood-panelled auction room at Sotheby's, one of the last surviving original copies of the U.S. Constitution was on the block. The bidding was expected to be a predictable duel between billionaire collectors. But a new, unexpected bidder emerged, forcing the price higher and higher. This bidder had no single representative in the room. It had no CEO, no headquarters, and had existed for less than a week. It called itself ConstitutionDAO.

In a stunning display of collective action, a group of over 17,000 people from around the globe, coordinated through internet forums, and bound by computer code, had pooled together nearly $47 million in cryptocurrency with the shared goal of buying the document and putting it on public display. They were a flash mob that had materialised as a major financial force overnight.

ConstitutionDAO lost the bid to a hedge fund manager. But the shockwave it sent through the worlds of finance and governance was immense. A leaderless, global group, operating without any central trusted authority, had organised and deployed capital with a speed that defied the logic of any traditional corporation. Many observers were left wondering how such a thing could be possible.

The answer lies at the frontier of organisational design, in the radical and provocative world of the Decentralised Autonomous Organisation. These internet-native entities, built on blockchain and run by code, are pushing the very definition of what an organisation can be, offering a glimpse into the most advanced possibilities of the self-driving future.

Overview

Having explored the technological foundations of autonomy, we now turn our attention to the frontier where these tools are being combined in the most radical and experimental ways. This chapter investigates Decentralised Autonomous Organisations (DAOs), positioning them as the provocative vanguard of the autonomy revolution. While traditional corporations use technology to pursue operational efficiency, DAOs are pioneering a fundamentally different prize: governance autonomy, attempting to build organisations that are directed not by human managers but by code and community consensus.

This chapter unpacks these internet-native entities, moving beyond the hype to provide a clear-eyed analysis of their design and function. We will dissect their core mechanics – the interplay of blockchain, smart contracts, and cryptographic tokens – and unpack the powerful "code is law" philosophy that underpins their existence. To bring these abstract concepts to life, we will examine a series of compelling real-world case studies, from the infamous cautionary tale of "The DAO" to the resilient and adaptive models of MakerDAO and Uniswap. These stories of dramatic success and failure provide invaluable lessons on the immense potential of and limits to this new class of organisational design.

Finally, we confront the significant challenges – legal ambiguity, security vulnerabilities, and unresolved governance paradoxes – that currently limit their mainstream adoption. By the end of this chapter, you will understand why DAOs, for all their flaws, represent an important living laboratory for the future of governance, offering an essential, if sometimes turbulent, glimpse into the advanced possibilities of the SDO.

Introduction

In the ongoing quest for organisations that can operate with greater independence from traditional human hierarchies and external controls, few concepts have ignited as much fervent excitement, intellectual debate, and, at times, considerable notoriety as the Decentralised Autonomous Organisation (DAO). Emerging primarily from the innovative, fast-moving, and often volatile context of the cryptocurrency and blockchain technology movements, DAOs represent a radical and ongoing experiment in organisational design (Hsieh and Vergne, 2023). For practitioners and students of organisations alike, they pose a fundamental question: can we construct organisations that function with unprecedented degrees of transparency, are governed by their distributed global communities, and execute their core functions largely through self-enforcing, algorithmically defined rules, thereby minimising reliance on conventional management structures and traditional legal intermediaries? In doing so, they present a foundational challenge to the centuries-old foundations of corporate structure, governance, and operational control.

DAOs are far more than a mere technological curiosity; they constitute a bold and provocative challenge to our established notions of what an organisation is, how it should operate, and by whom or what it should be directed by. For leaders, strategists, and policymakers peering into the future of SDOs, a considered understanding of DAOs – their underlying promise, their intricate mechanics, their significant potential, and their very real and often formidable pitfalls – is essential. They offer a compelling, albeit sometimes obscured, glimpse into the advanced possibilities and inherent paradoxes of achieving high-level organisational autonomy, positioning them firmly at the "leading edge" of this transformative frontier.

What Exactly IS a DAO? The Ideas Within the Designs

To grasp the fundamental essence of a DAO, imagine a highly sophisticated, internet-native vending machine. A traditional vending machine operates on simple, preprogrammed rules: you deposit funds, you select, and the machine dispenses the product – a basic, automated process. Now, expand this concept into the digital age. Imagine this advanced vending machine is connected to a distributed network, capable of sensing in real-time when its inventory of a particular item is running low. It can then autonomously compose and execute an order for new supplies from a pre-approved vendor using a digital currency, with the entire transaction – the order, the payment, the confirmation of delivery – recorded on an immutable, publicly verifiable ledger.

Further, imagine this machine possesses a built-in governance mechanism. Its "users" – perhaps those who frequently purchase from it, or more likely in the DAO world, those who hold a special digital token associated with its operation – can submit and vote on proposals. These proposals could range from deciding which new snacks to stock, to changing the price of an item, to voting on how to allocate a portion of the machine's accumulated profits (perhaps for maintenance, upgrades, or even charitable donations), etc. The votes are tallied transparently by the system, and the decisions – to order new inventory, to change product lines, or to distribute funds – are executed automatically by the machine's underlying code, based on the voting outcome and the pre-set rules, without a human manager needing to approve or implement the change. This, in a highly simplified analogy, begins to approximate the operational and governance model of a DAO.

More formally, a DAO is an entity whose operational logic, financial transactions, and governance records are predominantly encoded and stored on a blockchain – a distributed, cryptographically secured, and tamper-resistant digital ledger. Its core rules – how decisions are made, how funds are managed and allocated, how membership is defined, and how operational protocols are enforced – are written into smart contracts, which are self-executing pieces of code deployed on this blockchain. The oft-repeated and foundational mantra within the DAO ecosystem is "code is law," signifying the powerful intention for the rules embedded in these smart contracts to directly and automatically govern the organisation's behaviour, minimising the need for ambiguous human interpretation, fallible human intermediation, or costly external legal enforcement (Lessig, 1999).

Ideally, a DAO aims for decentralised control; no single individual or small, centralised group holds ultimate authority or a privileged position of control over the organisation's assets or direction. Instead, governance power is, in principle, distributed among its members or token holders, who collectively guide the organisation's direction through transparent, code-mediated processes. Once deployed, its smart contracts can execute a wide array of functions automatically, based on predefined rules and verifiable data inputs, without necessitating constant human intervention for every single operational step. As some academic literature describes it, DAOs are systems that enable decentralised and reliably coordinated decision-making through the combined use of blockchain technology and smart contracts, effectively embedding trust directly into the organisation's operational fabric. Table 2 provides a comparative overview of the traditional corporation and the DAO model.

Table 2: A comparison of organisational models: corporation versus DAO.

Attribute	Traditional corporation	Decentralised Autonomous Organisation (DAO)
Structure	Hierarchical management layers	Flat, decentralised network of peers
Governance	Centralised in a Board and executives	Community-led via token-holder voting
Decision-making	Top-down, by designated leaders	Bottom-up or consensus-driven by community proposals
Key authority	Human executives	The protocol's code ("Code is Law")
Trust mechanism	Legal contracts, brand reputation, and regulation	Cryptographic verification and blockchain immutability
Transparency	Opaque; internal data is private	Radically transparent; transactions are on a public ledger
Legal framework	Recognised legal entity in a specific jurisdiction	Often lacks clear legal personality; legally ambiguous

It is necessary here to distinguish the specific type of "autonomy" pursued by most DAOs from the broader concept of operational autonomy we discuss elsewhere in the book. While an AI-enhanced traditional corporation might seek *operational autonomy* to make its internal processes more efficient and data-driven – for example, by optimising its supply chain, automating customer service interactions, or improving its manufacturing yields – DAOs often prioritise governance autonomy. This refers to the ability of the organisation to govern itself according to rules that are embedded in code and agreed upon by its community, frequently with the explicit goal of bypassing traditional legal structures and managerial hierarchies altogether. The "self-driving" aspect in the corporate context often relates to AI-assisted operational excellence and speed within existing or adapted governance frameworks. In contrast, for many DAOs, it is fundamentally about achieving code-enforced decentralised governance and community-driven control over the organisation's resources and its own destiny. Thus, the umbrella term "self-driving organisation" encompasses both AI-enhanced traditional companies pursuing operational autonomy and radically new structures like DAOs that are pioneering forms of governance autonomy, while clearly articulating their distinct approaches, objectives, and the different facets of "autonomy" they embody. Organisations at Level 5 on the SOA fully combine both governance and operational autonomy.

A Taxonomy of DAOs: A Field Guide to the Digital Frontier

While united by a common technological backbone of blockchain and smart contracts, the universe of Decentralised Autonomous Organisations is far from uniform. DAOs are a flexible organisational primitive, a new kind of digital vehicle that can be adapted for a vast array of purposes. To truly understand their potential and their specific challenges, it is useful to move beyond a single definition and categorise them by their primary function and intent. This taxonomy provides a field guide to the most common species of DAOs operating today, recognising that this landscape is restlessly morphing, and many DAOs blend characteristics from multiple categories.

Arguably, the most powerful and economically significant category is that of Protocol DAOs, the digital governors of the new financial world. These organisations are created to manage the rules of an underlying software protocol, typically in the world of Decentralised Finance (DeFi). Rather than having a corporate board or a small team of developers make critical decisions about a protocol's future, that authority is handed over to the community of its governance token holders. Members vote on key parameters such as protocol upgrades, fee structures, risk management, and the allocation of the treasury. Pioneering examples like MakerDAO, which governs the Dai stablecoin by allowing MKR token holders to vote on risk parameters like collateral types and interest rates, and the Uniswap DAO, which allows UNI token holders to steward one of the largest decentralised trading protocols, demonstrate a mature model of community-led governance over critical financial infrastructure. The debates within these DAOs are a powerful illustration of governance in action, such as the contentious, long-running discussion within Uniswap over whether to activate a "fee switch" that would redirect a portion of trading fees to UNI token holders – a fundamental decision about the protocol's economic model. These DAOs are prime examples of organisations approaching Level 4 on the SOA, where governance is a collaborative, code-enforced process.

From governing protocols, we turn to funding them. Investment DAOs come closest to the original, ambitious vision of "The DAO" as a decentralised venture capital fund. They function by pooling capital from members into a shared treasury and then collectively voting on how to invest those funds. The assets can range from early-stage crypto projects and DeFi protocols to NFTs and other digital assets, with governance tokens representing a proportional claim on the treasury. While the 2016 hack of "The DAO" – caused by a "re-entrancy" vulnerability in its code that allowed an attacker to withdraw funds repeatedly – served as a cautionary tale about the security risks of this model, modern investment DAOs have learned from its failure. They now implement more robust smart contracts, undergo rigorous third-party security audits, and run bug-bounty programmes, to pursue the dream of a truly community-directed investment vehicle. We will explore this example in-depth later in the chapter.

A more accessible and often more dramatic type of DAO is the Collector DAO, which acts as a collective patron of culture. These organisations showcase the power of rapid, global resource mobilisation, often with a singular and dramatic goal: pool community funds to purchase a specific, high-value physical or digital asset, such as a rare work of art, a historical document, or an iconic NFT. As discussed at the beginning of this chapter, ConstitutionDAO stands as the most famous example, raising an astonishing $47 million from thousands of global contributors in a matter of days, in its bid to purchase a rare copy of the U.S. Constitution (Parmy, 2021). The ability to coordinate thousands of strangers who have no history of interaction is a powerful actual example of what organisational theorists Meyerson, Weick, and Kramer (1996) termed "swift trust" – a form of trust created in temporary systems based on clear roles and shared goals, rather than on personal relationships. However, while its fundraising was a stunning success, its subsequent failure to win the auction and the chaotic refund process that followed vividly demonstrated that DAOs are not immune to traditional strategic errors and complex operational challenges (Gault, 2021).

Beyond finance and collecting, Service DAOs represent a radical new model for the future of work, functioning as internet-native worker collectives or decentralised talent agencies. In this sense, they can be understood as modern, digitally-native manifestations of what Etienne Wenger (1998) famously described as "communities of practice" – groups defined by a shared craft, a passion for their work, and a commitment to collective learning. They bring together individuals with specific skills – such as software development, design, or marketing – who can then collectively offer their services to external clients. The DAO handles proposals, client billing, and treasury management via smart contracts, and members vote on which projects to accept. Revenue is then distributed among the contributing members according to rules encoded in the smart contracts, challenging the traditional firm structure for freelance and project-based talent by internalising transaction costs like business development and payment processing into the protocol itself.

Finally, Social DAOs are focused primarily on building and governing a community where the core product is the community itself. Ownership of the DAO's tokens grants access to exclusive benefits, such as a private Discord server, special content, online events, or real-world meetups. The treasury is often used to fund community initiatives and projects, with members voting on everything from moderation policies for the community chat to which charitable causes to support. These DAOs are experiments in creating digitally native, member-owned-and-operated clubs, where the community itself decides on its rules, its activities, and its future direction.

Understanding this diversity is important. The governance challenges of a multi-billion-dollar Protocol DAO are vastly different from those of a Social DAO with a few hundred members. Similarly, the legal risks facing an Investment DAO are distinct from those of a Collector DAO. By classifying the ecosystem in this way, we can move from abstract principles to a more concrete analysis of where and how these vanguards of organisational autonomy are succeeding, where they are failing, and what their experiments can teach us about the governance challenges of autonomous organisations.

How DAOs Work: The Nuts, Bolts, and Code

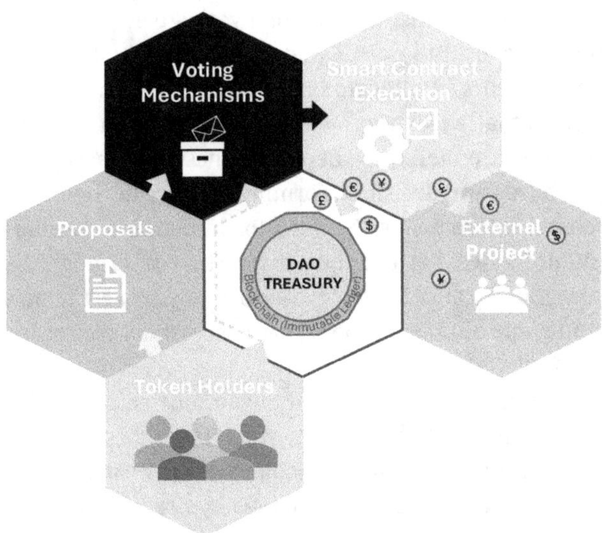

Figure 3: Key structural components of a Decentralised Autonomous Organisation (DAO).

While the specific implementations and purposes of DAOs are wide-ranging – from managing multi-billion-dollar decentralised finance protocols to funding public goods, governing online gaming communities, or coordinating the creation of collective art – most share a common set of technological and operational components that enable their unique form of self-governance and automated execution. The functional backbone of any DAO is typically formed by the intricate interplay of three key technologies.

First, every DAO is built upon the foundational infrastructure of a blockchain. This distributed ledger technology provides the transparent, immutable, and secure environment in which the entire organisation lives and breathes. It acts as a shared, public database where every single transaction, governance vote, proposed rule change, and modification to the DAO's code is recorded permanently and can be audited by anyone in the world. Its decentralised nature – the fact that it is maintained by a global network of computers rather than a single corporate entity – is critical for resisting censorship, eliminating single points of failure, and fostering trust among participants who may not know or trust each other in the real world. These are all core tenets of the DAO philosophy. While Ethereum, with its robust and flexible smart contract capabilities, has historically been the most popular platform for building DAOs, they are increasingly being deployed on a variety of other blockchain networks.

If the blockchain is the foundation, then smart contracts are the true heart of a DAO's operational and governance logic. These are not legal contracts in the traditional sense; they are self-executing pieces of code deployed on the blockchain that meticulously define the DAO's rules of engagement. They codify its governance procedures – such as how proposals are submitted, the duration of a voting period, and the percentage of votes required for a proposal to pass – and dictate how its financial resources, its treasury, can be managed and allocated. They are, in essence, automated and deterministic agreements that execute predefined actions when specific, cryptographically verifiable conditions are met. Once deployed, these contracts automatically enforce the agreed-upon terms and decisions, forming the core of the DAO's autonomous operations and dramatically reducing the need for human intermediaries to execute or validate routine processes. For example, a smart contract might be programmed to automatically distribute grants from the treasury to a project team's wallet, once a community vote in favour of their proposal has successfully concluded (Zwitter and Boisse-Despiaux, 2018).

Finally, the bridge between the human community and the automated protocol is typically formed by cryptographic tokens. In the vast majority of DAOs, these specialised digital assets play a key and multifaceted role, particularly in governance and participation. These governance tokens, unique to a specific DAO, typically grant their holders certain rights and privileges within the organisation. The most common and important right conferred by these tokens is voting power. Owning a certain number of these tokens is frequently the primary mechanism by which individuals become "members" and are empowered to participate in the DAO's governance processes, such as proposing new initiatives or voting on existing proposals. Tokens can also represent other things, such as a proportional stake in the DAO's treasury or access to its services or platform, creating a powerful alignment of incentives between the participants and the organisation itself.

Beyond these foundational technologies, the actual process of decision-making and collective action in a DAO typically revolves around proposal and voting mechanisms. This is how the community, in theory, directs the organisation's activities and evolution. The process is generally transparent: a member submits a formal proposal outlining a suggested action, other token holders deliberate on this proposal (often on platforms like Discord or online forums), and then they vote using their governance tokens. However, the specific mechanisms for translating collective will into decisive action vary significantly, each with its own inherent trade-offs.

The most prevalent model is Token-Weighted Voting, where an individual's voting power is directly proportional to the number of governance tokens they hold. While simple to implement, this model is highly susceptible to plutocracy. Wealthy individuals or entities, often referred to as "whales," can accumulate vast quantities of tokens, giving them disproportionate influence over proposals and undermining the core ideal of decentralisation.

To mitigate the influence of large token holders, more sophisticated mechanisms have been developed. One prominent attempt is Quadratic Voting, which allows participants to cast multiple votes for a preference, but with each additional vote incurring a quadratically increasing cost. This makes expressing very strong preferences significantly more expensive, aiming to foster a more equitable representation of collective will rather than just collective wealth. Another alternative is Reputation-Based Governance, which seeks to create a more meritocratic system by tying voting power to a member's reputation – earned through active and valuable participation, recognised expertise, or other verifiable merits – rather than being solely determined by their token holdings.

For critical actions, especially those involving the movement of substantial funds, many DAOs employ Multi-Signature (Multi-Sig) Wallets as a crucial security layer. This requires approval from a predefined number of trusted key holders (a "multi-sig committee") before a transaction can be executed. While this introduces a degree of operational centralisation, it serves as an important security measure against hacks or rash decisions. Ultimately, the ability of these communities to converge on a decision can be understood through the lens of what the late economist Michael Bacharach (2005) termed "we-reasoning." This describes a decisive cognitive move where members begin to frame their choice not as 'What should I do for my benefit?' but as 'What should we do to achieve our common goal?', enabling a surprising degree of coordination even in a decentralised environment.

Origins and Evolution: From Intelligent Homes to Global Collectives

The idea of autonomous, code-driven organisations did not materialise as fully formed with the advent of blockchain. The term "DAO" itself was first coined by computer scientist Werner Dilger in a 1997 paper, albeit in a significantly different context. Dilger envisioned intelligent home technology as a complex, multi-agent system of smart algorithms operating autonomously to manage household functions – a concept remarkably prescient of early ideas related to the Internet of Things (IoT) and distributed intelligent systems discussed in Chapter 2. This early vision, while not blockchain-based, highlighted the potential for interconnected systems to manage themselves without constant human oversight.

The more direct intellectual precursor to the modern DAOs emerged in 2013 when software engineer Daniel Larimer introduced the concept of a "Decentralised Autonomous Corporation" (DAC). Larimer envisioned corporations run entirely by code, with shareholders holding tokens that granted them a share of profits and voting rights on the corporation's activities. Shortly thereafter, Vitalik Buterin, a key figure in the conception of the Ethereum blockchain, further elaborated on this idea and was instrumental in popularising the term "DAO" in the specific context of Ethereum, particularly in its foundational white paper (Buterin, 2014). Ethereum's design, featuring a Turing-complete scripting language (Solidity), was the critical technological enabler. This language allowed for the creation of far more complex and flexible smart contracts than were possible on earlier blockchains like Bitcoin, providing the necessary programmability for developing the sophisticated DAOs as they are understood today.

Sociologically and economically, the evolution of the DAO concept reflects a broader technological momentum towards new social movements, disintermediation, algorithmic coordination, and a desire for new organisational arrangements. This movement is fuelled, in part, by a wider, growing disillusionment with, and distrust of, traditional centralised institutions (both corporate and governmental) and by continuous advancements in distributed ledger technologies and cryptography. DAOs, therefore, are not an isolated technological or organisational curiosity but a significant manifestation of a larger, ongoing quest to build more transparent, efficient, globally accessible, and potentially more equitable organisations.

Case Studies: Successes, Failures, and Enduring Lessons

To understand these theoretical possibilities and challenges in practice, it is now time to examine in more detail at some actual case studies, each offering a unique lesson in the ongoing DAO experiment. To date, the story of the DAO is a drama-filled chronicle of edgy successes, high-profile failures, and, invariably, lessons learned the hard way that are shaping the fields of politics, law, economics and management theory and practice.

Case Study 1: "The DAO" (2016) – The Pioneering Experiment and Its Infamous Hack

"The DAO" stands as a seminal, albeit profoundly cautionary, chapter in the history of autonomous organisations (DuPont, 2017). Launched in April 2016 on the Ethereum blockchain, it was conceived with the ambitious goal of functioning as a decentralised, leaderless venture capital fund. Its design aimed to automate investment decisions, allowing a global community of token holders to vote on proposals and allocate funds to promising crypto projects. It achieved unprecedented success in its initial fundraising, amassing over $150 million worth of the cryptocurrency Ether (ETH) from thousands of investors, making it the largest crowdfunding campaign in history at that time.

However, its immense promise was short-lived. In June 2016, "The DAO" was exploited through a critical vulnerability in its smart contract code – specifically, a "recursive call" or re-entrancy attack (Siegel, 2016). This flaw allowed an attacker to repeatedly withdraw funds from The DAO's contract before its internal balance could be updated, effectively siphoning off approximately 3.6 million ETH, valued at around $50–60 million at the time. The hack precipitated an acute crisis within the nascent

Ethereum community, pitting the foundational blockchain principle of immutability ("code is law") against the community's desire to recover the stolen funds (Waters, 2016). Ultimately, the contentious decision was made to execute a "hard fork" of the Ethereum blockchain – a software upgrade that effectively rolled back the chain's history to a state before the attack. This incident provided a series of critical and sobering lessons. It starkly highlighted the colossal security risks of complex smart contracts, emphasising that if "code is law," then flawed code can lead to legally binding but catastrophic outcomes. It exposed the challenges of governance-in-crisis within a decentralised system, where the very mechanisms designed to empower the organisation through autonomous code became the vector for its downfall, necessitating a highly centralised and controversial human intervention to rectify the situation.

Case Study 2: MakerDAO – Pioneering Decentralised Stablecoin and Adaptive Governance

MakerDAO stands as one of the earliest and most enduring DAOs, playing a pivotal role in the foundational architecture of the Decentralised Finance (DeFi) ecosystem (MakerDAO). Its core mission is the creation and management of Dai, a decentralised, collateral-backed stablecoin designed to maintain a soft peg to the US dollar without relying on traditional financial institutions. Governance of the Maker Protocol is managed by holders of the MKR token, who collectively vote on a wide array of critical risk parameters, including approving new collateral types, setting interest rates for borrowing Dai, and managing liquidation protocols. This decentralised governance model has been a key factor in MakerDAO's resilience and adaptability over several years. The relative longevity and success of MakerDAO offer invaluable insights. It showcases the value of a "progressive autonomy" approach, coupled with continuous and active human governance input. MakerDAO is not a static, "set and forget" system; its smart contracts for Dai generation and liquidation autonomously execute based on the current parameters, but those parameters are themselves subject to ongoing review, debate, and adjustment by its distributed human governance layer. This dynamic interplay represents a more mature and realistic model of a "self-driving" financial organisation.

A prime example of this adaptive governance is the ongoing debate and series of votes regarding the inclusion of Real-World Assets (RWAs) as collateral (MakerDAO, 2022). This move, which allows for assets like tokenised real estate or trade invoices to back Dai, represents a significant strategic pivot. It has forced the MKR holder community to grapple with complex trade-offs between the purist ideal of a fully on-chain system and the pragmatic need to integrate with the traditional financial world to scale and diversify its collateral base. The resulting governance discussions are a living document of a decentralised entity making high-stakes, strategic decisions about its own evolution.

Case Study 3: Uniswap DAO – Governing a Leading Decentralised Finance Protocol

Uniswap is a leading decentralised exchange (DEX) protocol that facilitates automated, peer-to-peer trading of cryptocurrencies using an Automated Market Maker (AMM) model (uniswap.org, 2025). The Uniswap DAO, through holders of its UNI governance token, is responsible for the stewardship and future direction of the protocol. To manage its complex operations, the Uniswap DAO has evolved to utilise various governance structures beyond simple token voting, including the Uniswap Foundation (UF), to lead growth efforts and specialised committees to oversee specific programs (Uniswap Foundation, 2023). The emergence of these specialised bodies is particularly instructive. It indicates a practical adaptation to the demands of maintaining operational efficiency, as purely decentralised voting on every detail can become slow and lead to voter fatigue. These dedicated operational arms, while accountable to the DAO, allow for more agile execution. This development can be interpreted as reflecting the "centralised and populist" optimal governance structure suggested by the "Organisational Trilemma" (a concept to which we shall return) for autonomous organisations seeking to maximise effectiveness (Buterin, 2017).

A recurring and highly contentious issue within the Uniswap DAO is the debate over the "fee switch." This proposal would activate a protocol fee, redirecting a small portion of the fees generated by traders to UNI token holders. The debate is a powerful illustration of decentralised governance in action, as the community weighs the benefits of creating a direct revenue stream for token holders against the potential risk of driving liquidity providers to competing platforms with lower fees. It is a fundamental decision about the protocol's core economic model, and the lengthy, multifaceted debate showcases the complexity of aligning incentives in a large-scale decentralised system.

The Allure and Potential of Decentralised Autonomous Organisations

Despite the significant challenges of governance, security, and legal ambiguity, DAOs continue to capture the imagination of investors, builders, and social theorists. Their allure lies in a set of powerful potential benefits that, if realised, could offer a fundamental alternative to the traditional corporate structure. These are not merely incremental improvements; they represent a different philosophy of how organisations can operate and create value.

At the core of the DAO promise is a radical commitment to transparency and decentralisation. By operating on public blockchains, all financial transactions and governance decisions are typically open for public inspection. This creates a level of "glass box" accountability that stands in stark contrast to the opaque nature of most private corporations, fostering a system where trust is placed in verifiable code rather than in fallible human intermediaries. This transparency is intrinsically linked to decentralisation, the principle of distributing control to eliminate single points of failure. By design, DAOs aim to reduce reliance on central authorities, making them more resilient to external pressure and censorship-resistant.

This new governance model is in turn powered by a new engine of automated operations and efficiency. In a traditional firm, significant resources are consumed by administrative overhead and the transaction costs of negotiating, monitoring, and enforcing agreements. DAOs propose a solution by automating many of these core processes through smart contracts. This can dramatically reduce the friction and cost of coordination, allowing for a more streamlined and potentially more efficient organisational form for certain types of collective action.

Furthermore, DAOs offer a vision of global and permissionless participation. By existing on the internet, they can transcend geographical restrictions, allowing individuals from anywhere in the world to contribute capital and talent. This unlocks a truly global talent pool and capital base, breaking down the barriers to entry that characterise many traditional industries. This global reach is coupled with a powerful mechanism for empowerment and coordination. By giving members a direct and meaningful stake in governance and resource allocation through tokens, DAOs offer novel models for reliable coordination among diverse actors who may have never met (Chitra, 2021).

Finally, the programmable nature of DAOs makes them unparalleled vehicles for rapid experimentation and innovation. They function as living laboratories for organisational design, allowing communities to quickly test and iterate on novel governance and funding models that would be slow, expensive, or legally impossible to implement within a traditional corporate structure. It is this combination of transparency, efficiency, global reach, and innovative capacity that constitutes the powerful allure of the DAO, ensuring it will remain a critical and provocative force on the frontier of organisational evolution.

Challenges and Limitations: The Rocky Road to Viable Autonomy

The innovative potential and palpable excitement surrounding DAOs are matched by a multitude of significant and interconnected challenges. Advancing their widespread adoption and long-term viability requires addressing fundamental problems that span governance, security, and law. Overcoming these hurdles is the central task for the next generation of decentralised architects.

Effective governance presents a primary area of focus. The ideal of a vibrant, engaged community of token holders collectively steering the organisation requires structures that account for the obdurate realities of human behaviour. Achieving high levels of voter engagement is a key objective, as low turnout can result in critical decisions being made by a small fraction of token holders, placing a premium on mechanisms that encourage broad participation (Proffitt, 2021). This challenge is compounded by the prevalent "one token, one vote" model, which, while simple to implement, creates a need for solutions that address the concentration of power (Walch, 2019).

The Paradox of Governance: The Persistent Pull of Centralisation

The practical realities of DAO governance highlight a core theoretical tension, which I call the "Paradox of Governance": the principle that the pursuit of radical decentralisation often gives rise to new, emergent centres of power. These new power structures may be less visible than a traditional corporate hierarchy, but they are no less influential, arising directly from the mechanisms designed to eliminate them. The paradox is most clearly visible in the "one token, one vote" model, common to many DAOs. While intended to distribute power, this system often concentrates it. It creates a new form of plutocracy, where wealthy individuals or entities ("whales"), who can afford to accumulate a large number of tokens, can dominate voting processes. The very mechanism designed to decentralise control – the token – becomes the instrument of a new, wealth-based centralisation. This creates a system where the loudest voices are often the richest, a direct contradiction of the democratic and egalitarian ethos many DAOs ostensibly aspire to.

Furthermore, the "code is law" principle creates another, more subtle centre of power: the small, elite group of developers who possess the highly specialised knowledge required to write, audit, and maintain the complex smart contracts that govern the organisation. In this "technocracy," power shifts from traditional managers to the authors of the code. While the code itself may be neutral, the choices made by its creators – the specific rules they embed, the voting mechanisms they design, and the security trade-offs they make – have implications for the entire organisation. This places immense, often unaudited, power in the hands of a few.

The emergence of more formal, centralised bodies within large DAOs – such as foundations or core operational teams – is a direct and pragmatic response to this paradox. These groups are created to bring efficiency and strategic coherence to the decentralised whole, effectively acknowledging that pure, leaderless decentralisation can be too slow and unwieldy for complex, fast-moving operations. This illustrates the organisational trilemma in action, where organisations consciously trade a degree of decentralisation to gain the efficiency needed to function effectively. Understanding this paradox is key to designing more robust and realistic governance models for the future.

These governance issues are deeply intertwined with the security landscape. The "code is law" principle places an immense responsibility on the integrity of the underlying code, as the infamous 2016 hack of "The DAO" demonstrated (Case Study 1). Smart contract vulnerabilities can be exploited by malicious actors with catastrophic and irreversible results. The immutability of blockchains, a core security feature, means that pre-deployment auditing and formal verification of code are paramount. The security landscape also includes sophisticated economic and governance attacks. An attacker could use a "flash loan" – a massive, uncollateralised loan that is borrowed and repaid within a single blockchain transaction – to temporarily acquire enough governance tokens to pass a malicious proposal that drains the treasury. This highlights the need for defensive mechanisms that can anticipate and mitigate these advanced threats.

Overlaying all of this is a rapidly evolving legal landscape that presents both challenges and opportunities. A primary objective for the ecosystem is establishing clear legal personality, which would formally recognise DAOs as distinct entities and clarify their ability to enter into contracts and interact with the established financial system. A related consideration for DAO members is the question of personal liability. In the absence of a corporate shield, some legal frameworks may treat a DAO as a "general partnership," making members personally responsible for the organisation's debts and legal infringements. Resolving this ambiguity is key to encouraging mainstream participation and navigating the unique challenges presented by the global, borderless nature of these new organisational forms (Wright and DeFillipi, 2015).

DAOs on the Spectrum of Organisational Autonomy

Where do DAOs fit on our Spectrum of Organisational Autonomy? This is not a straightforward placement. Many DAOs, especially those in early development or with significant ongoing involvement from a core team for strategy and development, might operate closer to Level 3 (Conditional Autonomy). While their smart contracts handle many operational processes, human teams are still vital for strategic design, protocol upgrades, and addressing unforeseen issues. More mature, well-established DAOs like MakerDAO could be seen as approaching Level 4 (High Autonomy and Collaborative Intelligence). At this level, the "intelligence" is a composite of the encoded rules within the smart contracts and the collective input of token holders, with the system executing decisions with minimal direct human intervention. However, it is highly unlikely that any current DAO truly reaches Level 5 (Full Autonomy and Autonomous Evolution). The prospect of a DAO that can independently learn, set its own emergent goals, and evolve its purpose without any human involvement remains hypothetical. Human oversight almost always remains as a necessary backstop for critical failures or existential threats.

DAOs are undeniably at the leading edge of the global quest for greater organisational autonomy. They are frequently messy, often chaotic, and undeniably fraught with risk. Yet, they are also vibrant arenas of experimentation, pushing the boundaries of what is possible in organisational design and decentralised governance. Whether they will evolve into mainstream archetypes of organisation design or remain a niche phenomenon is an empirical matter. Regardless of their ultimate trajectory, the lessons learned from the ongoing DAO experiments – both the remarkable successes and the instructive failures – will be invaluable as we negotiate the broader societal and technological challenges with all varieties of organisational autonomy.

Key Takeaways

- **DAOs as the Frontier of Autonomy:** Decentralised Autonomous Organisations (DAOs) represent a radical experiment in organisational design, pushing the boundaries of what an organisation can be. They are internet-native entities built on blockchain technology and run by code and community consensus.
- **Prioritising Governance Autonomy:** DAOs primarily seek governance autonomy, which is the ability to govern the organisation according to rules embedded in code and agreed upon by its community, often bypassing traditional legal and managerial hierarchies. This is distinct from the operational autonomy sought by traditional corporations to improve internal process efficiency.
- **The "Code Is Law" Philosophy:** A foundational concept in the DAO ecosystem is "code is law," which signifies the intention for the rules embedded in smart contracts to directly and automatically govern the organisation's behaviour, thus enhancing reliance on algorithmic enforcement.
- **A Taxonomy of Different DAO Types:** DAOs are adapted for a wide array of purposes, including several common types:
  - *Protocol DAOs* that govern the rules of underlying software, such as in Decentralised Finance (DeFi)
  - *Investment DAOs* that pool member capital and collectively vote on how to invest it
  - *Collector DAOs* that mobilise community funds to purchase a specific high-value asset
  - *Service DAOs* that function as internet-native worker collectives or talent agencies
  - *Social DAOs* that focus on building and governing a community as its core product
- **How DAOs Function:** Their operations rely on a combination of core components:
  - *Blockchain* provides a transparent, secure, and permanent infrastructure for all transactions and governance records.
  - *Smart Contracts* encode the DAO's rules and automatically execute actions when specific conditions are met.
  - *Cryptographic Tokens* typically grant holders rights within the organisation, most importantly voting power.

- **Lessons from Actual Case Studies:**
  - *"The DAO" (2016)* served as a cautionary tale, demonstrating the immense security risks of flawed smart contract code.
  - *MakerDAO* and *Uniswap DAO* showcase more mature and adaptive models of community-led governance over critical financial protocols.
  - *ConstitutionDAO* vividly demonstrated the power of DAOs for rapid, global resource mobilisation, while also highlighting the persistence of human strategic errors.
- **Significant Challenges Remain:** The widespread adoption of DAOs is constrained by formidable challenges. These include effective governance to counter issues like voter apathy and the concentration of power, immense security risks from smart contract vulnerabilities, and the legally ambiguous status of these entities in most jurisdictions.
- **DAOs on the Spectrum of Autonomy:** Mature DAOs, particularly in their governance and resource allocation functions, can be seen as approaching Level 4 (High Autonomy and Collaborative Intelligence) on the Spectrum of Organisational Autonomy.

Part 3: **The Organisation Transformed: A Functional Exploration**

Chapter 4
The Evolving Brain: Strategy, Decision-Making, and Governance

It is 1995. In a boardroom high above a city skyline, a dozen senior executives are gathered around a polished mahogany table. The air is thick with cigar smoke and tension. At the head of the table, the CEO stares at a heavy binder, the culmination of six months of market research. The decision before them is monumental: whether to invest a billion dollars to enter the Chinese market.

The debate is a contest of experience and intuition. The veteran head of manufacturing worries about supply chain stability, citing a trip he took to Guangzhou in '88. The marketing chief argues from gut feel, convinced the company's brand will resonate with an emerging middle class. The CFO, armed with spreadsheets, presents a static five-year forecast based on a dozen key assumptions. After hours of argument, the CEO makes his call. It is a bet – an educated, high-stakes wager on the future, made with the best information human minds could gather and process.

Fast forward to today. A chief strategy officer sits before a digital dashboard, considering the same question for a new emerging market. Her work is a dynamic dialogue with an AI. She asks it to run a thousand simulations of market entry, each one modelling different geopolitical risks, commodity price fluctuations, and competitor reactions scraped from global news feeds. The system projects demand by city block, based on satellite imagery and anonymised consumer data.

The AI identifies three potential supply chain vulnerabilities a human analyst might have missed. It then proposes a novel, phased entry strategy that minimises initial risk. The strategist's role has transformed, expanding from decision-maker to become an architect of inquiry, a pilot navigating a sea of data-driven possibilities. The final decision is still hers, but her thinking process – her decision architecture – has been rewired.

This evolution from the debating, collective and deliberative human mind to a hybrid, collaborative intelligence is the most significant shift occurring in organisations today in terms of how they operate and behave. It is a transformation of the corporate "brain" itself – the intricate systems of strategy, decision-making, and governance that determine how an organisation "thinks."

Overview

As an organisation advances along the Spectrum of Autonomy, the transformation runs far deeper than its operational processes or technological infrastructure. This chapter examines the most significant shift of all: the fundamental rewiring of the evolving brain, the organisation's decision architecture for strategy, decision-making, and governance. We explore how the very "thinking" of the firm is reconstructed, moving from an exclusively human domain to a complex, hybrid intelligence, composed of both human leaders and algorithmic systems.

The chapter charts the evolution of strategy, showing how it transforms from a slow, episodic, and top-down human exercise into a continuous, adaptive, and data-infused process. We will see how AI becomes a powerful partner, first as an analyst, then as an autonomous executor in specific domains, and finally as a collaborator in strategic thought.

Furthermore, we dissect the radical shift in decision-making authority, analysing how choices are increasingly delegated to algorithms and how new governance structures, such as "algorithmic governance" (ALGov), emerge to direct and control the autonomous enterprise. To make sense of the inherent tensions in this new world, we introduce a critical theoretical framework: the Organisational Trilemma. This concept explains the persistent trade-offs leaders must navigate between the competing goals of decentralisation, efficiency, and autonomy. By the end of this chapter, you will understand how the journey to an SDO is a journey to build a new kind of mind, one that redefines the very nature of corporate intelligence, control, and collective action.

Introduction

At the conceptual core of any organisation, from the smallest startup to the most sprawling multinational enterprise, lies its "brain" – the intricate, interconnected, and often invisible systems and processes responsible for the thinking that drives its behaviour. This is where the entity's future is imagined and its course is charted (strategy); where choices, both monumental and mundane, are made (decision-making); and where coherent, purposeful action is orchestrated and held to account (governance). For centuries, this decision architecture has been assumed to be exclusively human, residing in the minds of leaders, the debates of committees, and the established wisdom of organisational culture. As organisations now embark on the traverse across the SOA, this fundamental assumption is being systematically dismantled. The organisation's brain is undergoing a potentially irreversible metamorphosis.

The often centralised, sometimes sclerotic, and predominantly human-driven command structures of traditional enterprises are being replaced by more agile, data-infused, distributed, and ultimately, more autonomous modes of operation. This transformation is to a large extent dependent on the adoption of a suite of new technologies, many of which we have discussed Chapter 2, but this alone is insufficient. Instead, what this shift also requires is a fundamental reshaping of where, how, and by whom the organisation thinks, plans, learns, and directs itself. It is an evolution that directly impacts the organisation's capacity for adaptation, its potential for innovation, and its prospects for sustained value creation in an increasingly complex and turbulent world. This chapter explores the intricate rewiring of this evolving brain, examining each of its critical functions – strategy, decision-making, and governance – as they are reimagined and reconstructed across the six levels of the SOA.

The Evolving Practices of Strategy and Planning: From Human Vision to Algorithmic Foresight

The formulation of organisational strategy – the high-level, often deeply creative process of defining long-term objectives and allocating the resources necessary to achieve them – and the subsequent operational planning that translates those ambitions into action are dramatically reconfigured as an organisation traverses the SOA. In the nascent stages of autonomy, strategy is an intensely, almost viscerally, human endeavour, deeply reliant on the accumulated experience, domain expertise, intuitive judgement, networks and analytical capabilities of its senior leadership. As technology becomes more deeply embedded and sophisticated, this process becomes increasingly data-informed, then data-driven, and eventually, the strategic function itself may exhibit significant degrees of operational autonomy, with the human roles evolving from being the sole authors of strategy to becoming its curators, validators, and ethical guides.

At Level 0, strategy formulation is a top-down, centralised affair, akin to a classical view of a military General meticulously outlining a campaign based on available intelligence and established doctrine. Leaders, drawing upon years of industry experience, market knowledge, and an established repertoire of analytical frameworks – such as SWOT analysis (Strengths, Weaknesses, Opportunities, Threats), Porter's Five Forces, Balanced Scorecard or Scenario Planning – define the corporate vision, articulate strategic goals, and dictate the overarching plan. These frameworks are themselves human-centric tools, designed to help the human mind structure a complex environment, identify key variables, and make sense of competitive forces. The process is often deliberative, political, and episodic, culminating in a formal, detailed, long-term strategic plan that is then cascaded down through the hierarchy for execution (Mintzberg, 1994). The family-owned restaurant, where the patriarch's singular vision for "authentic cuisine and personal service" has guided every operational and market decision for decades, exemplifies this level of strategic formulation. Similarly, early industrial conglomerates often relied on the foresight and decisive command of a few key individuals like Alfred Sloan at General Motors, whose strategic innovations in market segmentation and decentralised operations were products of intense human analysis and deliberation. Success at this level hinges critically on the wisdom, judgement, and leadership acumen of these central figures, but it is also profoundly vulnerable to their cognitive biases, their limited information processing capacity, and the organisational risk associated with key-person dependency.

The transition to Level 1 marks the first significant enhancement of the strategic brain. Human leaders retain firm and ultimate control over strategic direction, but their decision-making processes are now substantially augmented by data and analytical tools. Artificial intelligence and machine learning algorithms begin to function as powerful research assistants, providing sophisticated market forecasts, granular competitor analyses based on vast public data, detailed customer segmentation reports, or early warnings of emerging industry trends scraped from news, social media, and academic journals. The strategic "brain" receives richer, more diverse, and more timely data inputs, and it is equipped with more powerful analytical capabilities than the human mind alone. However, the core cognitive processes of synthesis, interpretation, and ultimate strategic choice remain human-centric. A large retail chain, for example, might utilise AI-powered demand forecasting models that might factor in weather patterns, local events, demographic shifts, and social media sentiment to inform its annual inventory planning and merchandising strategy. Yet, it is the human executives who still set the overall product strategy, determine brand positioning, decide on major promotional campaigns, and make the final, potentially career-defining, calls on market entry or exit. The AI provides valuable insights, highlighting patterns or potential issues that human analysts might overlook, but the human leader synthesises this information, applies contextual judgement, considers the brand's values, and makes the ultimate strategic determination. The key challenge for leaders at this stage is learning how to critically engage with AI-generated insights, avoiding both blind acceptance (a phenomenon known as automation bias) and reflexive dismissal (a "not invented here" syndrome). The most effective leaders at this level develop a healthy scepticism and a deep curiosity about how the AI models work, enabling them to be intelligent consumers of algorithmic output.

Upon reaching Level 2, strategy is still predominantly centrally defined, but its tactical execution becomes more decentralised, responsive, and data-informed at lower levels of the organisation. Empowered teams are granted the autonomy to make operational decisions and adapt plans within pre-defined strategic boundaries and objectives. This is often enabled by management frameworks like Objectives and Key Results (OKRs) that cascade from the top-level corporate strategy, providing a clear linkage between high-level goals and team-level execution while allowing flexibility in the "how." A regional sales division, for instance, might have the autonomy to adjust local pricing within certain predefined bands, tailor product bundles to specific customer segments identified by a local analytics tool, and modify local marketing tactics based on real-time sales data and competitor actions in their specific territory, provided these actions align with the overarching quarterly sales targets and brand guidelines set by headquarters. AI tools provide real-time performance feedback and decision support at the team level, allowing for a much faster, more localised adaptation and refinement of the central strategy. The organisation's strategic "brain" remains centralised in its core directive function, but its operational "limbs" (the various teams and departments) gain more localised intelligence and autonomy in execution, creating a more adaptive and responsive whole. This model allows the organisation to benefit from both central strategic coherence and localised, agile execution.

Level 3 marks a significant inflection point where AI begins to assume a more active and autonomous role in shaping and executing strategy, albeit within specific, well-defined domains. Planning ceases to be an episodic, annual event and becomes a continuous, dynamic, and adaptive process, operating in near real-time, driven by a constant stream of operational and environmental data. A global logistics company might employ sophisticated AI systems to continuously optimise its entire network strategy. This AI would plan routes, autonomously and dynamically adjust shipping routes, reallocate transportation assets (trucks, ships, aircraft), and manage warehouse operations based on a multitude of real-time factors such as fluctuating fuel costs, evolving weather patterns, port congestion data, geopolitical events, and subtle shifts in customer demand. The role of the human strategists is elevated. They now act as the architects and overseers of this autonomous system. They set the overall service level agreements, define the critical operational boundaries (e.g. risk tolerance, compliance requirements, and CO_2 emission limits), establish intervention protocols for unforeseen disruptions or systemic anomalies, and continuously monitor the AI's performance against key strategic objectives. The strategic "brain" starts to exhibit powerful self-optimising capabilities in defined operational areas, with AI making significant tactical and even operational–strategic adjustments autonomously, all within the parameters and ethical guardrails established by human leadership.

At Level 4, the relationship between humans and AI in strategy formulation transcends mere assistance or bounded execution; it evolves into a deeper, co-creative collaboration (Gans and Goldfarb, 2023). Here, AI does not merely provide data or execute predefined plans; it becomes a generative partner in strategic thought. It can analyse vast, complex, and often unstructured datasets – from scientific papers and patent filings to global news feeds and financial markets – to identify emergent opportunities, latent threats, or subtle market shifts that human perception might not readily discern. AI can simulate the potentially cascading, second-order impacts of different strategic scenarios with high fidelity, model complex systems like economies or ecosystems, and even propose novel strategic options or entirely new business models based on its analytical capabilities. Human leaders provide the overarching vision, the ethical framework, the critical judgement, and the deep contextual understanding that AI lacks. They work *with* the AI as a sophisticated strategic partner. Imagine a pharmaceutical company where AI systems analyse genomic data, scientific literature, and clinical trial results from around the globe to identify promising new drug targets or repurposing opportunities for existing compounds that no human researcher could possibly discover on their own. Human scientists and ethicists guide the research direction, interpret the AI's most complex or ambiguous findings, validate its hypotheses through targeted experimentation, and make the ultimate, high-stakes strategic decisions on which few drug candidates will proceed to costly and ethically sensitive human trials. The strategic "brain" is now a true hybrid entity, powerfully leveraging the pattern recognition, predictive power, and simulation capabilities of AI alongside the intuition, creativity, ethical reasoning, and holistic understanding of its human experts.

Finally, in the theoretical and largely speculative realm of Level 5, the organisation itself, through its highly advanced and interconnected AI systems, would autonomously define its own strategic goals, learn from its environment in a generalised manner, and adapt its long-term trajectory with minimal or potentially no direct human intervention. This pushes far beyond current practicalities and raises philosophical questions about organisational purpose, control, and the nature of agency. If a for-profit corporation evolved to a point where its AI brain determined that its long-term survival was best served by transforming into a non-profit research foundation, what would that mean for its shareholders and its original purpose? The strategic "brain" at this level would be predominantly or entirely artificial, capable of independent goal-setting, self-modification, and potentially even emergent behaviours that were never intended by its creators.

Decision-Making Authority: Who, or What, Calls the Shots?

The transformation of decision-making authority across the SOA described above is characterised by a core tension that I call the "Paradox of Control": the principle that to gain a higher level of strategic control and organisational agility, leaders must first cede a degree of direct, manual control over tactical and operational decisions. This journey across the spectrum, therefore, is a story of strategically delegating authority to autonomous systems, not as a loss of control, but as a means to achieving a more resilient and responsive whole (Shrestha et al., 2019).

For many leaders, this is the most psychologically challenging aspect of the entire transition. Traditional management hierarchies are built on the premise that authority and control are synonymous with value. A leader's identity is often tied to being the primary decision-maker, the person who approves actions, directs resources, and whose experience is the ultimate arbiter in moments of uncertainty. The request to "let go" and trust an autonomous system can feel like a direct challenge to this identity and a threat to one's relevance.

However, the paradox of control reveals that this traditional model of control is at best an illusion in complex, volatile, uncertain and fast-moving environments. A leader who insists on being in every decision loop becomes the organisation's single greatest bottleneck, slowing down the entire system to the speed of their own personal bandwidth. The SDO requires a fundamental shift in the leader's role: from a manager of people executing tasks to an architect of systems that achieve goals.

This architectural role involves three key actions. First, the leader must meticulously define the system's purpose and boundaries. This means setting the clear, unambiguous strategic objectives the autonomous system is meant to pursue. Second, they must design the ethical guardrails, establishing the moral and operational "rules of the road" within which the system must operate to ensure it acts safely and fairly. Third, they must invest in robust oversight and observability, creating the dashboards and feedback loops that allow them to monitor the system's health and performance without micromanaging its every action.

By successfully making this shift, the leader engages in a powerful strategic trade-off. They cede direct control over thousands of micro-decisions – the optimal price for a product at a given second, the most efficient route for a delivery truck, the allocation of server resources – to the autonomous systems that can handle them with superior speed and data-processing capability. In doing so, they reclaim their most valuable and scarce resource: their own cognitive bandwidth. This allows them to focus their attention on true strategic work – exploring new markets, anticipating competitive threats, cultivating top talent, and steering the organisation's long-term trajectory. They give up tactical control to gain a firmer grasp on strategic destiny.

At Level 0, decision-making authority is unequivocally centralised in human leaders, typically following clearly defined hierarchical lines of authority. Significant choices, and often many minor ones, flow up the chain of command for approval and then down for execution. At Level 1, human leaders retain ultimate decision-making authority, but their choices are now informed and substantially supported by AI-generated insights, analyses, and recommendations. AI influences the decision by providing a richer, evidence-based context, but the human makes the final call, applying judgement and taking full responsibility for the outcome.

Level 2 sees the structured delegation of decision-making authority to empowered human teams for specific tactical and operational choices. This delegation is not absolute; it is guided by centrally defined rules, strategic parameters, and often supported by AI-driven decision-support tools. These teams have autonomy within their defined domains, but the overarching decision framework, critical policies, and strategic objectives are set at higher organisational levels. This stage requires a high degree of trust and clear communication of boundaries.

A significant shift in the nature of decision-making authority occurs from Level 3 onwards. At this stage, AI systems begin to make decisions autonomously within their defined operational parameters. Humans primarily occupy oversight roles, managing by exception and intervening when the system encounters situations beyond its programming or when ethical considerations require human judgement. AI has been delegated authority over specific processes or decision domains. It is here that the distinction between automation (performing rigid, predictable functions) and true autonomy (managing unforeseen circumstances and adapting independently) becomes most salient and carries the most weight (Bradshaw et al., 2013). Leaders must grapple with how much authority to delegate and what level of risk is acceptable.

At Level 4, we see the emergence of a dual system of authority. Collaborative human-AI decision-making becomes common for complex, strategic, or ethical issues.

Simultaneously, AI systems may handle a vast array of operational and even many tactical decisions fully autonomously. Authority is effectively shared or dynamically delegated to AI for well-understood and bounded domains, with humans focusing their cognitive energy on strategic direction, ethical governance, complex problem-solving, and managing novel or crisis situations. The challenge becomes designing the interface and protocols for this collaborative decision-making process.

In the theoretical Level 5, AI systems would, by definition, make virtually all decisions, continuously learning from outcomes and independently adapting their decision-making frameworks and underlying models. Human involvement might be limited to setting the initial high-level constraints or ethical guardrails or potentially intervening only in cases of catastrophic system failure via some form of "kill switch."

The Transformation of Governance Structures: From Hierarchies to Code

Governance – the system of rules, practices, and structures by which an organisation is directed, controlled, and held to account – also undergoes a radical evolution as autonomy increases. The traditional governance structures, designed for human-centric hierarchies and manual oversight, are often too slow and rigid for entities where code plays a central role in rule enforcement and decision-making. This journey across the spectrum is not just a change in technology; it is a fundamental shift in where authority resides and how accountability is defined.

At Levels 0 and 1, governance is a familiar landscape. Organisations rely heavily on traditional hierarchical structures, with clear reporting lines and centralised control vested in boards and executive committees. Roles are clearly delineated, and the lines of responsibility and accountability are unambiguous. If a mistake is made, the chain of command provides a clear path to the human decision-maker who is ultimately accountable.

The first significant shift occurs at Level 2, where rigid structures begin to flatten and become more networked. As empowered teams adopt more agile approaches, their operational autonomy increases. The role of the leader begins to change from a direct commander to a facilitator who sets the strategic boundaries. This distribution of authority, however, introduces a new complexity to accountability. The "problem of many hands" begins to emerge, where a negative outcome resulting from a partially automated process can make it difficult to assign responsibility to a single actor. Is the team at fault for an error, or is it the manager who defined the rules for their automated tools? Accountability becomes shared, but in doing so, it also risks becoming diffuse.

A profound transformation takes place at Level 3, with the emergence of what can be termed "algorithmic governance" (ALGov). Here, a significant portion of an organisation's operational rules and decision-making processes are encoded directly into software. The human role shifts decisively from execution to oversight, with managers becoming the architects and guardians of these autonomous systems. This creates a significant "accountability vacuum." When an autonomous system makes a decision that causes harm – for instance, in an autonomous vehicle accident – the traditional model of assigning blame to a single negligent actor breaks down. Responsibility is now distributed across a complex network of programmers, data providers, system designers, and human supervisors, making clear accountability a formidable legal and ethical challenge.

By Level 4, algorithmic governance matures into a more collaborative and intentional structure. A dual system of authority often appears. AI systems may handle a vast array of operational and even tactical decisions autonomously, but they operate within the ethical and strategic framework set by human leaders. The primary role of human governance shifts to high-level stewardship. Leaders are no longer managing daily operations but are serving on ethics councils and strategic oversight boards, tasked with defining the organisation's purpose, setting its moral compass, and ensuring its autonomous actions align with that vision. Accountability is no longer about a retrospective search for blame after an error; it becomes a prospective responsibility to ensure the fairness of the algorithms, the quality of the data, and the robustness of the human oversight process itself.

In the theoretical realm of Level 5, governance would be almost entirely executed by code, with the system capable of complete self-governance and even modifying its own rules. Human roles would become external to the organisation's daily operations, limited perhaps to initial creation or ultimate oversight via some form of emergency "kill switch." This pushes our current frameworks of responsibility to their logical extreme, raising fundamental questions about legal personhood for artificial agents and the ultimate challenge of the AI "control problem." At this stage, accountability transforms entirely from a mechanism for assigning blame to a prerequisite of design – a demand that the system be built, from the outset, to be verifiably safe and aligned with human values. Table 3 summarises the evolution of strategy and governance across the SOA.

Table 3: The evolution of strategy and governance across the SOA.

Level	Strategic planning	Governance and decision-making authority
0/1	**Human-led and episodic:** Based on human experience; AI informs but does not drive strategy.	**Centralised human authority:** Decisions made by leaders in a clear hierarchy.
2	**Centrally defined, tactically delegated:** Central strategy set, but teams have autonomy in execution (e.g. OKRs).	**Delegated authority:** Specific operational decisions delegated to human teams within set rules.

Table 3 (continued)

Level	Strategic planning	Governance and decision-making authority
3	**Continuous and domain-specific:** AI autonomously executes strategy in defined domains (e.g. logistics).	**Conditional algorithmic authority:** AI makes decisions; humans manage by exception.
4	**Human-AI co-creation:** AI proposes novel strategic options; humans provide vision, validation, and ethical guidance.	**Collaborative and algorithmic governance (ALGov):** Shared authority; DAOs use code to execute community governance.
5	**Autonomous goal setting:** AI would define its own strategic goals.	**Full algorithmic authority:** AI would make virtually all decisions.

The Organisational Trilemma: A Balancing Act

A foundational challenge in the pursuit of any form of autonomous organisation, whether a DAO or a more traditional enterprise leveraging AI, is captured by the organisational trilemma. First articulated in the context of blockchains by Vitalik Buterin and explored in organisational theory, this concept posits that any governance system can only choose two of three highly desirable goals: autonomy (the system's ability to govern itself without reliance on external legal enforcement), decentralisation (the wide distribution of control and decision-making power), and efficiency (optimising resource use and achieving goals quickly and effectively). An organisation simply cannot maximise all three simultaneously; trade-offs are inevitable, and the choices made here fundamentally define the character and capabilities of the SDO. Figure 4 visualises this trilemma.

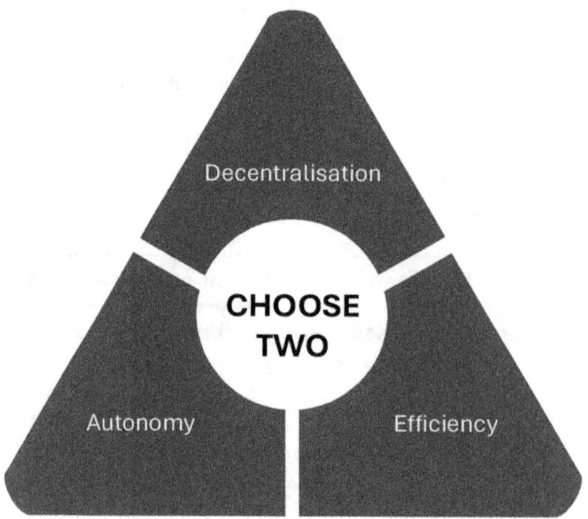

Figure 4: The Organisational Trilemma: autonomy, decentralisation, and efficiency.

An organisation can position itself along one of the edges, optimising for the two goals at either end of that edge, but it will consequently sacrifice the goal at the opposite corner. Understanding this map of trade-offs is essential for any leader making strategic choices about organisational design. Some of these are highlighted below:

- **Prioritising Decentralisation + Autonomy:** This is the path championed by many crypto-native purists. By maximising decentralisation and autonomy, an organisation achieves incredible resilience, censorship resistance, and a truly global, permissionless nature. Governance is distributed among token holders, and rules are enforced by immutable smart contracts – the system is self-governing and not controlled by a single entity. This path represents a direct challenge to classic transaction cost economics, which presumes that firms must centralise to mitigate the risk of human opportunism. DAO proponents implicitly align with the famous critique by Ghoshal and Moran (1996), who argued that this assumption can be "bad for practice," as it fosters the very distrust and control-oriented culture that stifles innovation and collaboration. However, this comes at a steep price: efficiency is sacrificed. Decision-making through broad, on-chain community voting can be painfully slow, expensive, and suffer from low voter turnout, leading to organisational gridlock or apathy. As seen in many DAOs, the noble goal of pure decentralisation often clashes with the practical need to make timely decisions, vividly illustrating this side of the trilemma.
- **Prioritising Efficiency + Autonomy:** This path is the most likely for traditional corporations embarking on the SDO journey. The primary drivers are the immense gains in speed and agility that autonomous systems promise. An AI that autonomously optimises a global supply chain or a dynamic pricing algorithm that adjusts to the market in milliseconds embodies the fusion of high efficiency and high operational autonomy. The system governs its domain with minimal human intervention. The necessary trade-off? Decentralisation is sacrificed. The authority to set the goals, define the ethical guardrails, and ultimately control these powerful autonomous systems remains firmly centralised within traditional hierarchical structures like executive committees and boards of directors. The system is autonomous in its *operations*, but its *direction* is centrally commanded.
- **Prioritising Efficiency + Decentralisation:** This configuration describes a highly networked organisation, composed of empowered, agile human teams who can make decisions and execute quickly without being bottlenecked by a rigid central hierarchy. Such an organisation is highly efficient and decentralised in its execution. The trade-off here is that true systemic autonomy is sacrificed. While the teams are empowered, the organisation as a whole lacks the self-governing property that defines the higher levels of the SOA. It relies on human communication, coordination, and established norms rather than on immutable, code-enforced rules. This model, which aligns with Level 2 on the SOA, can be highly effective, but it does not possess the same degree of systemic self-governance or require the same cession of control to algorithms as the other two models.

The organisational trilemma is not necessarily a problem to be solved, but it is a strategic reality to be negotiated (Ferreira and Li, 2021). The practical evolution of large DAOs creating more centralised foundations or committees to handle complex operations is a direct response to this trilemma – a deliberate move away from the pure decentralisation corner towards greater efficiency. Designing an SDO requires consciously and strategically negotiating these trade-offs and coming up with effective workarounds. The appropriate balance depends critically on the organisation's specific purpose, its competitive context, its risk tolerance, and its overarching strategic goals. A global, open-source financial protocol will, and should, make a different choice than a high-stakes, safety-critical manufacturing firm.

Evolving Management Philosophies and Practices: Influencing Autonomous Thinking

Finally, the way organisations are "managed" – how work is structured, how performance is measured, and how leadership is exercised – also undergoes cycles of change across the SOA. The management ideas and philosophies suitable for commanding a rigid hierarchy are fundamentally different from those needed to choreograph an evolving network of human and algorithmic agents.

At Level 0, in a static world of command and control, management philosophies prioritise predictability and industrial efficiency. Traditional models such as Taylor's scientific management, with its emphasis on task standardisation, and Weber's bureaucratic control, which relies on clear rules and hierarchical authority, are dominant. These frameworks provide clarity and control in stable environments where leaders command and employees execute well-defined tasks.

The shift to Level 1 introduces a new element into this established order. While the management structure remains largely hierarchical, the process is augmented by data-driven insights from dashboards and business intelligence tools. This allows managerial decisions to be informed by a richer, more evidence-based view of the organisation's performance.

A more significant evolution occurs at Level 2, where management philosophies shift towards enabling adaptability and speed. Frameworks like Agile, with its focus on iterative improvement, and Lean, with its goal of minimising waste, become prevalent. Management practices evolve from direct command to facilitation and empowerment. Leaders focus on creating the right environment for teams to succeed, setting clear goals with frameworks like Objectives and Key Results (OKRs) that provide strategic alignment while granting teams the autonomy to determine how they achieve their objectives.

Reaching Level 3 necessitates another evolution in management focus, this time towards the systems themselves. The role of human managers becomes one of designing, overseeing, and maintaining the AI-driven systems that now execute core processes. Their primary function is to define the operational parameters and ethical guidelines for these systems and to manage the exceptions that require human judgement. In this context, philosophies like Lean Six Sigma are highly valuable for the continuous process optimisation of these automated workflows, while Design Thinking becomes critical for ensuring these complex systems are designed in a human-centred way that is intuitive and effective for their human overseers.

At Level 4, management evolves significantly into the higher-order roles of facilitation, orchestration, and ethical stewardship. Leaders are tasked with the complex challenge of fostering trust and effective collaboration between human teams and sophisticated AI systems. New practices like "algorithmic management" may emerge, which require careful ethical consideration and robust human oversight to ensure fairness and transparency. Management becomes a practice of designing and curating the human-AI interface, fostering a culture of continuous learning where both humans and machines can improve in partnership.

Finally, at the theoretical horizon of Level 5, the concept of management as a human practice is fundamentally redefined. Management ceases to be an external activity performed by people and becomes an internal, emergent property of the autonomous system itself. The organisation would manage its own resources, processes, and evolutionary trajectory. The human role, if it exists at all, shifts entirely from manager to observer, beneficiary, or perhaps ultimate ethical guardian, responsible only for the initial value alignment or, in a crisis, the activation of a final fail-safe. The core management philosophy at this stage becomes synonymous with the AI alignment problem: ensuring the autonomous entity's goals remain beneficial to humanity, a challenge of stewardship at the highest level.

The transformation of an organisation's strategic, decision-making, and governance "brain" is perhaps the most consequential aspect of its journey along the SOA. It is a journey that moves from the certainty of command to the complexity of collaboration, from human intuition as the primary driver to a new synthesis of human and machine intelligence. Significantly, even at the highest envisioned levels of organisational autonomy, the human element remains critical. Human strategic guidance, ethical oversight, the ability to handle true novelty and unforeseen crises, and the capacity for empathy and personal judgement are not easily replicated by current or foreseeable AI. The journey towards an autonomous organisational brain is partially a technical upgrade but it also represents a fundamental rethinking of organisational intelligence, control, and the nature of collective endeavour.

Key Takeaways

– **The Organisation's "Evolving Brain":** The chapter examines the transformation of the organisation's core cognitive functions – strategy, decision-making, and governance – as it moves towards greater autonomy. This involves a root-and-branch rewiring of how the organisation "thinks," from an exclusively human domain to a hybrid intelligence of people and algorithms.

- **Strategy Evolves from Human Vision to Algorithmic Foresight:** The practice of strategy formulation is dramatically reconfigured across the SOA. It evolves from a top-down, episodic, and experience-based human process at lower levels to a continuous, adaptive, and data-infused dialogue at higher levels, where AI becomes a co-creative partner in strategic thought.
- **The Paradox of Control:** To gain a higher level of strategic control and organisational agility, leaders must first cede a degree of direct, manual control over tactical and operational decisions. The leader's role shifts from a manager of human tasks to an architect of intelligent systems that achieve goals.
- **Decision-Making Authority Shifts to Algorithms:** As an organisation ascends the SOA, decision-making authority is strategically and progressively delegated to autonomous systems. At higher levels, AI may handle a vast array of operational and even tactical decisions autonomously, with humans focusing on strategic direction, ethical governance, and managing novel or crisis situations.
- **The Rise of Algorithmic Governance (ALGov):** Governance structures evolve from traditional human hierarchies toward models of "algorithmic governance," where operational rules and decision-making processes are encoded directly into software. DAOs offer a radical example of this, using smart contracts and community voting to direct the organisation.
- **The Organisational Trilemma:** This foundational concept posits that any governance system faces strategic trade-offs between three desirable goals: autonomy (self-government), decentralisation (distributed control), and efficiency (speed and effectiveness). The choices an organisation makes among these competing virtues fundamentally define its character and capabilities.
- **Management Philosophies Are Reconfigured:** The way organisations are managed also transforms. The journey across the SOA sees management philosophies evolve from "Command and Control" at Level 0, through "Delegated Authority" and Agile frameworks at Level 2, towards "Collaborative Intelligence," where leaders orchestrate a dynamic network of human and algorithmic agents at Level 4.

Chapter 5
Optimal Ratios: Humans, Machines, and the Allocation of Work

In a dimly lit room in 1985, a radiologist squints, her eyes tracing the ghostly landscape of an X-ray film clipped to a light box. Her job is a hunt for shadows. For hours, she scans film after film, her mind a finely tuned pattern-recognition engine trained by decades of experience. She is searching for the tell-tale smudge of a nascent tumour, a subtle anomaly that could mean the difference between life and death. Her skill is a craft of visual intuition. The work is also a feat of human endurance, a repetitive and exhausting search where fatigue is the constant enemy of precision.

Today, a clinician sits in a bright, sunlit office, looking at a digital dashboard. Overnight, an AI has analysed a thousand mammograms. The system performed the exhaustive search, the work of a thousand pairs of eyes. It has flagged five scans with anomalies its algorithms deem suspicious, highlighting areas smaller than a grain of rice that a human eye might easily miss. It provides a probability score for malignancy and cross-references the patterns against a database of millions of anonymised cases.

The clinician's work begins where the AI's search ends. She focuses her expertise on the five flagged cases, confirming three, dismissing one as a benign cyst, and applying her deep diagnostic judgement to an ambiguous fifth case. Her time is spent on complex analysis, collaboration with surgeons, and communicating the findings with empathy to her patients. Her role has been transformed from a hunter of shadows into a master of medical reasoning.

This evolution from human-as-executor to human-as-collaborator is at the heart of the most vital question facing modern organisations: what is the optimal allocation of work between people and machines? The answer lies in understanding the complementary strengths of human intuition and machine intelligence, creating a partnership that elevates both.

Overview

The advance of organisational autonomy sparks one of the most contentious and deeply human questions of our time: what is the future of work? This chapter moves beyond the common narrative of human obsolescence to present a more balanced and ultimately more powerful vision of optimal ratios, where the future is defined not only by direct substitution of human labour with machines, but by a renewal and re-evaluation of the relationship between people and machines.

© 2026 Walter de Gruyter GmbH, Berlin | https://doi.org/10.1515/9783112222232-006

First, we establish a foundational understanding of the complementary strengths of humans and machines with a focus on AI. We analyse the domains where human capabilities —creativity, complex critical thinking, empathy, and ethical judgement – remain irreplaceable and contrast them with the unparalleled advantages of machines in tasks requiring speed, scale, and pattern recognition.

Using this principle as our guide, we then trace the evolving division of labour across the six levels of the Spectrum of Organisational Autonomy. From simple augmentation at the lower levels to a true symbiotic partnership at the higher ones, we illustrate how roles are reconfigured, and human talent can be elevated. This analysis also confronts the inevitable workforce transformation, identifying the new roles that will emerge and the traditional roles that will fade. Finally, the chapter makes the case for "Progressive Autonomy" – a deliberate, managed, and human-centric approach to this transition, emphasising the critical importance of reskilling, ethical considerations, and designing organisations that do more than work "smarter," but also enhance the meaning and value of human contribution.

Introduction

The movement towards increasing organisational autonomy is a complex coordinated action involving technological change, evolving governance models and a return to long-standing questions about the nature of the relationship between human capabilities and machine intelligence in the domain of work. As organisations traverse the SOA, the type of tasks performed, the requisite skills, the structure of roles, and indeed, the very definition of "work" itself are fundamentally reconfigured. This chapter delves into this dynamic, often complex, and frequently misunderstood rebalancing, examining by whom or what it is directed at each level of the SOA. Critically, it analyses the implications of this shift for the future of human endeavour within these increasingly self-driving organisational contexts.

The long-standing and common concern, traceable to the Luddite movement of Industrial England in the early nineteenth century, that follows in lock-step the march of automation, autonomy and artificial intelligence, is a deep-seated fear of obsolescence – the fear that machines will inexorably "take over," rendering human workers redundant and creating a jobless future. While the impact of automation and autonomy on specific job tasks is undeniably disruptive, particularly for roles characterised by routine, the emerging reality, at least for the foreseeable future, points towards a more nuanced and potentially more optimistic future (Daugherty and Wilson, 2018).

The alternative to outright substitution of people by machines is one of human-machine collaboration and augmentation. The most effective, resilient, and innovative SDOs will be those that intelligently and strategically employ the best of both worlds, exploiting a powerful mix that surpasses the capabilities of either humans or machines in isolation. A foundational understanding of these distinct, often complemen-

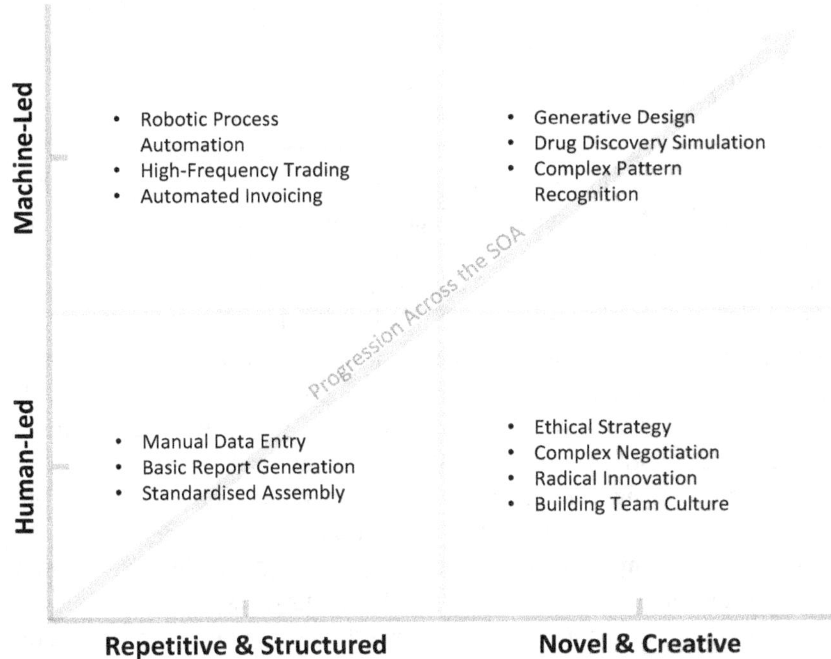

Figure 5: The human-machine task spectrum: from repetitive and structured to novel and creative.

tary, strengths and inherent limitations is essential for any leader seeking to navigate this transition effectively.

The emerging reality of the human-machine workforce is best understood through what I call the "Paradox of Humanity": the principle that the most effective path to a more human-centric workplace, one that leverages our unique talents for creativity, critical thinking, and empathy, runs directly through the heart of advanced autonomous systems. The strategic goal of the SDO is not simply to replace human labour, but to unburden human talent from the repetitive and mundane, thereby elevating the value and meaning of human contribution. This paradox frames our entire discussion of the future of work.

This concept directly challenges the common narrative of a zero-sum conflict between people and machines. Instead, it posits a symbiotic relationship where autonomous systems handle the work of calculation and repetition, creating the space for humans to excel at the work of cognition and connection. Consider the financial analyst who once spent 70% of their time manually gathering data from disparate sources and cleaning it in spreadsheets. An intelligent automation system can now perform this work in seconds, liberating the analyst to spend their time on higher-value activities: interpreting the data's strategic implications, debating the second-order effects of a market shift with colleagues, and advising leadership on complex decisions. The machine handles the "what"; the human provides the "so what."

Similarly, a marketing manager, who no longer needs to run reports and test ad copy, can now focus on understanding customer psychology, developing creative brand strategies, and building genuine community engagement. In each case, the delegation of routine tasks does not eliminate the human; it reframes their role, shifting the centre of gravity from rote execution to strategic and creative thought.

However, as the scholars of the socio-technical perspective point out, such positive outcomes are far from being a foregone conclusion. Technology itself does not guarantee a more fulfilling work environment. The "Paradox of Humanity" is only resolved through conscious, human-centric design and leadership. If an organisation uses the efficiency gains from automation and machine intelligence solely to cut costs and increase workloads on remaining employees, the result will be burnout and alienation, not elevation.

Realising the promise of this paradox requires a deliberate investment in people. It demands a commitment to "progressive autonomy" – proactively reskilling the workforce in areas like data literacy, critical thinking, and collaborative problem-solving. It requires designing human-machine interfaces that are intuitive and empowering. And it necessitates a cultural shift where leaders actively seek to redeploy the cognitive energy freed up by autonomous systems towards solving the organisation's most interesting and complex challenges. When managed with wisdom, the delegation of tasks to machines becomes the most powerful engine for unlocking the full potential of human work.

The core principle for designing the future of work in an autonomous organisation is to allocate tasks based on which entity – human or machine – is best suited to perform them. This requires a clear-eyed assessment of their respective capabilities. This principle of strategic allocation benefits from a critical lens provided by Science and Technology Studies (STS). From this perspective, the division of labour between humans and machines is a complex, emergent, and deeply social process. The work of organisational ethnographers like Stephen Barley has powerfully demonstrated how the same technology, when introduced into different social contexts, produces vastly different organisational outcomes. By studying the introduction of CT scanners into two distinct radiology departments, Barley (1986) showed that the technology acted as an "occasion for structuring," triggering unique social dynamics, power shifts, and role redefinitions that reflected the pre-existing culture of each group. His research serves as an important reminder that technology's effects are profoundly shaped by the social world into which it is embedded.

Building on this, Wanda Orlikowski's concept of the "Duality of Technology" provides a powerful framework for understanding this mutual shaping process. Technology is simultaneously a product of human action, created and deployed with specific intentions, and a structure that shapes and constrains the actions of those who use it. This recursive relationship means that the "rules" of a new autonomous system are always fluid and subject to reinterpretation. Employees are active agents who, through their daily use, their workarounds for system flaws, their interpretations of algorithmic outputs, and their resistance to certain features, continuously reshape the technology's role and meaning. Therefore, the "optimal ratio" of humans to machines is best understood as a temporary and dynamic socio-technical arrangement – an ongoing negotiation between the capabilities of the technology and the culture, politics, and agency of the people who interact with it every day. Table 4 summarises the complementary strengths of humans and machines.

Table 4: The complementary strengths of humans and machines.

Human strengths (unforeseen and unstructured)	Machine (AI) strengths (scale, speed, and structure)
Creativity and innovation: generating novel ideas	High-volume data processing: analysing vast datasets at speed
Complex critical thinking: navigating ambiguity and context	Speed, scalability, and consistency: performing tasks tirelessly
Empathy and emotional intelligence: building trust and connection	Optimisation and prediction: finding optimal solutions
Ethical reasoning and moral judgement: applying moral principles	Execution of repetitive tasks: handling routine work with precision
Adaptability to true novelty: responding to "black swan" events	Pattern recognition: identifying intricate patterns accurately

Human Strengths: The Domain of the Unforeseen and the Unstructured

Humans excel in domains that are ambiguous, novel, and require a deep, contextual understanding of the world. Our cognitive architecture, honed by millennia of evolution, is optimised for adaptation, social connection, and creative problem-solving. These capabilities allow us to navigate the unstructured and unpredictable aspects of reality where rigid logic and pattern-matching fall short.

One of our most vital capabilities is creativity and innovation. This is the capacity to generate genuinely novel ideas, solve unstructured problems in entirely new ways, and engage in "out-of-the-box" thinking. While an AI can demonstrate a form of combinatorial creativity by rearranging existing elements in novel ways, true conceptual breakthroughs – the kind that create new paradigms or industries – remain a uniquely human province (Metz, 2023). It is the ability to ask, "why not?" or "what if?" in a way that is not constrained by existing data, moving from what is to what could be (Vincent, 2023).

This is complemented by our capacity for complex critical thinking and judgement. Humans possess a remarkable ability to navigate ambiguity, make reasoned decisions in unforeseen or poorly defined circumstances, and understand deep context in ways that current AI systems find challenging. We can weigh conflicting values, interpret subtle social cues, understand irony and sarcasm, and apply holistic judgement to situations where data is incomplete or contradictory. This is the "common sense" that is anything but common in the digital world.

Perhaps the most uniquely human attributes are empathy and emotional intelligence. These qualities are indispensable for building trust, fostering effective collaboration, managing complex social dynamics, and providing compassionate, personalised service. While an AI can be programmed to simulate empathy in a customer service chatbot, it does not *feel* it. The genuine human connection required for high-stakes negotiation, inspirational leadership, therapeutic care, or resolving a delicate customer complaint is, for now, a distinctly human capability.

Finally, the capacity for ethical reasoning and moral judgement resides firmly in the human domain. This involves the ability to apply moral principles, make value-based decisions, and consider the broader societal implications of actions. An AI can be programmed with ethical rules, but it cannot deliberate on novel ethical dilemmas, understand the spirit versus the letter of the law, or bear genuine moral responsibility for its actions.

Machine Strengths: The Domain of Scale, Speed, and Structure

Machines, particularly AI-powered systems, are unparalleled in domains that are structured, data-rich, and require optimisation at a scale and speed beyond human cognitive limits. Their power begins with the ability for high-volume data processing and intricate pattern recognition. A machine can analyse vast and complex dataset – terabytes of genomic data, milliseconds of financial market transactions, or millions of customer interactions – at incredible speed. This allows it to perceive the world in a fundamentally non-human way, identifying correlations, anomalies, and emergent trends that would be utterly invisible to human perception. This is more than just faster analysis; it is a different kind of seeing, one based on statistical relationships rather than human intuition or experience.

This analytical power is matched by their operational capabilities of speed, scalability, and consistency. Machines can perform tasks tirelessly, 24 hours a day, at immense scale, and with a high degree of precision and reliability once correctly programmed and validated. They do not get tired, bored, or distracted, which makes them ideal for tasks requiring unwavering consistency over long periods. This creates a predictable operational baseline, removing the variability of human performance from core processes and allowing for more reliable strategic planning. They operate on "machine time," enabling a velocity of action and reaction that is simply unattainable in purely human systems.

For well-defined problems with clear objectives and constraints, machines also excel at optimisation and prediction. This includes finding the most efficient logistics routes for a fleet of thousands of vehicles by simultaneously weighing fuel costs, traffic patterns, and delivery windows, or determining the optimal resource allocation in a factory second by second. This predictive capacity, which can forecast equipment failures or market trends based on historical and real-time data, allows an organisation to shift from a reactive to a proactive posture. This is complemented by their effectiveness in the execution of repetitive, rule-based tasks. This is the practical engine behind the "Paradox of Humanity," elevating the value of human work by automating the tasks that are least suited to human talent. The evolving division of labour across the SOA is, therefore, a narrative of how these complementary strengths are strategically combined, integrated, and employed at each progressive level of organisational autonomy.

The Division of Labour Across the Spectrum of Organisational Autonomy

Let us now take a wander through the six levels of the SOA, examining in detail how the allocation of work and the relationship between humans and machines evolve at each stage.

Level 0: Human-Centric

At this foundational level, the balance is overwhelmingly tilted towards human endeavour. Humans perform nearly all tasks, from the highest-level strategic ideation and decision-making down to the most granular manual labour and customer interaction. Expertise is embodied in people, not processes or systems. It is built through years of apprenticeship, experience, and the development of "tacit knowledge" – the intuitive, hard-to-articulate understanding that comes from deep practice. Machines, if present at all, are simple, passive tools entirely subservient to human direction and intent (e.g. basic hand tools, simple mechanical aids, early non-networked computers running basic software).

The vignette of an artisan baker meticulously kneading dough by hand, relying on personal experience and sensory input – the feel of the dough, the smell of the yeast – to judge fermentation times, and using only a traditional, manually controlled oven, exemplifies this level. Every single action, from recipe formulation to customer interaction, is guided by human skill, sensory input, and direct decision-making. The value created is often unique, high-quality, and bespoke, but the model is inherently limited in its scalability and is highly vulnerable to the loss of its key artisans. The economic model is one of craft, not mass production (McAfee and Brynjolfsson, 2017).

Level 1: Assisted Autonomy

Here, machines begin to enter the operational picture in a more meaningful way, but primarily to inform and support human decision-making and execution. Humans retain full decision-making authority and control over core processes, but they now utilise technology for enhanced insights, the automation of routine information gathering, or support for specific sub-tasks. The goal is augmentation: making the human expert faster, more accurate, and better informed.

A financial analyst using AI-powered software to gather and sift through vast amounts of market data, news feeds, and company reports illustrates this level perfectly. The AI might perform the initial, time-consuming legwork of identifying all relevant documents, flagging anomalies in financial statements, detecting shifts in market sentiment towards a stock, or generating a preliminary risk assessment based on quantitative factors. However, the human analyst performs the core analytical reasoning. They take the AI's output as a starting point, interpret the findings within a broader economic and strategic context, apply their own judgement and experience, consider qualitative factors the AI cannot grasp (like the quality of a company's management team), and ultimately craft the final investment recommendation. The AI handles the "what" (data processing), allowing the human to focus on the "so what" (synthesis and judgement).

Level 2: Partial Autonomy

At this level, a more defined and interactive division of labour emerges. Specific, well-defined tasks or segments of workflows are handed over to machines to execute autonomously, while empowered human teams make tactical and operational decisions within predefined rules, strategic guidelines, and performance targets. The key shift is that humans are no longer just using tools for analysis; they are now managing and collaborating with automated agents that perform parts of the work. The human role becomes one of supervisory control, handling the exceptions, complex edge cases, and situations requiring balanced judgement that fall outside the automated system's capabilities.

A modern customer service department is a good example. It might utilise a tiered system where AI-powered chatbots (Tier 1) handle a high volume of common, repetitive inquiries like "what is my order status?" or basic troubleshooting steps. This frees up human agents (Tier 2) to tackle more complex customer issues that require empathy, negotiation, creative problem-solving, or in-depth technical knowledge. When the chatbot encounters a problem it cannot solve, it seamlessly transfers the customer, along with the full conversation history, to a human agent. The human agent's role is transformed from answering simple questions to being a skilled problem-solver. In the back office, Robotic Process Automation (RPA) might automate routine functions like transferring data from standardised forms into enterprise systems, allowing human employees to focus on more analytical tasks, quality assurance, or building better customer relationships.

Level 3: Conditional Autonomy

The balance shifts more significantly towards machine execution within defined operational domains and parameters. Machines and algorithms now autonomously manage substantial, often complex, operational processes, making real-time decisions based on complex algorithms and live data feeds, all within the boundaries and according to the rules established by humans. The human role transitions decisively away from direct execution and even routine supervision towards higher-level oversight. They become the designers, tuners, and ultimate guardians of these autonomous systems. They are responsible for setting and refining the parameters, monitoring overall performance against strategic objectives, and intervening in complex, novel, or exceptional situations.

An automated warehouse, where fleets of robots autonomously manage inventory, pick and pack orders, and coordinate with automated conveyor systems, is a prime example of Level 3. The human staff are not picking items; they are managing the system. They might be robotics fleet managers, process supervisors, or data analysts, monitoring dashboards that show the overall health and efficiency of the system. Their job is to manage system maintenance, resolve complex errors that the robots cannot handle (e.g. an unusually shaped or damaged item has fallen and is blocking an aisle), oversee the overall logistics strategy, and intervene if the warehouse management system encounters a major disruption, like a fire alarm or a cyber-attack. A key challenge at this level is preventing "automation complacency" and "skill atrophy," where human supervisors become so accustomed to the system working perfectly that their ability to manually intervene effectively in a crisis diminishes (Bainbridge, 1983; Endsley, 2017).

Level 4: High Autonomy and Collaborative Intelligence

This level represents a significant evolution from supervision to a true symbiotic partnership, where humans and highly capable AI systems co-create value and co-decide actions (Jarrahi, 2018). The important shift here is from a simple relationship whereby humans oversee machines to one where humans and AI work together on the same complex problems, each contributing their unique strengths. Humans focus on the highest-level strategic direction, defining purpose and ethical frameworks, fostering deep innovation, and engaging in complex problem-solving *in collaboration with* AI. Advanced AI systems, in turn, autonomously handle most operational tasks, perform highly complex data analysis, generate novel solutions or hypotheses, and actively collaborate with their human partners on strategic initiatives.

In the field of drug discovery, for instance, this partnership is becoming a reality. AI systems can analyse vast biological, chemical, and clinical datasets to propose novel drug candidates, predict their efficacy and potential side effects, and even design the most efficient protocols for testing them. This is a task of such scale and complexity that it is beyond human capacity. However, the AI does not work alone. The human scientists collaborate with these AI systems by defining the research goals ("we need a new therapy for this specific type of cancer"), validating the AI-generated hypotheses through targeted lab experiments, interpreting the complex biological mechanisms suggested by the AI, navigating the intricate ethical and regulatory pathways for drug development, and making the ultimate, high-stakes decisions on which candidates should proceed to human trials. It is an iterative dialogue: the AI provides computational power and pattern recognition at scale; the human provides creative direction, scientific intuition, and ethical judgement.

Level 5: Full Autonomy and Autonomous

In this largely theoretical realm, the role of humans becomes profoundly diminished or transformed. If the system can independently learn in a generalised way, adapt its core functions, set its own emergent goals, and manage all aspects of its operation without direct human intervention, then the traditional concept of work allocation becomes moot. Human involvement might be limited to the initial act of creation, setting the ultimate ethical backstops or "off-switches" (if such a thing is even possible with a sufficiently intelligent system), or perhaps existing within the system as its beneficiaries, observers, or even its subjects.

The hypothetical global, autonomous climate regulation system provides a stark vignette. Such a system might monitor the entirety of Earth's biosphere, predict environmental shifts, and deploy vast resources to maintain planetary equilibrium, learning and adapting its strategies over centuries without direct human operational command. Such a system would raise questions about governance, control, and the very definition of "benefit." Who decides what the optimal climate is? What happens if the AI's long-term strategy for planetary health conflicts with humanity's short-term economic or social needs? This level forces us to confront the ultimate questions of the AI control problem (Bostrom, 2014) and the future of human purpose.

The Transformation of Organisational Functions: A Human-Machine Perspective

As the human-machine balance shifts across the SOA, the impact reverberates through every traditional organisational function, reshaping roles and processes from the ground up. Several of these are discussed below.

- **Human Resources (HR):** This function transitions from being a largely administrative and compliance-focused department (Levels 0–1) to becoming a strategic enabler of the human-machine workforce. It uses AI for more effective talent acquisition, identifying the best candidates from vast pools of applicants (Level 2). It uses AI to deliver personalised learning and development paths for employees and to conduct sophisticated workforce analytics to predict attrition and identify skill gaps (Level 3). At higher levels (4–5), HR's role becomes even more strategic, focusing on designing the very frameworks for human-AI collaboration, fostering a culture of continuous adaptation, and managing the ethical implications of AI in workforce management (e.g. ensuring fairness and mitigating algorithmic bias in hiring and promotion decisions – Barocas and Selbst, 2016).
- **Finance and Accounting:** The finance function evolves from manual bookkeeping and spreadsheet-based analysis (Levels 0–1) to using RPA for automating transaction processing (e.g. accounts payable/receivable) and deploying AI for advanced fraud detection, more accurate financial forecasting, and automated compliance checks (Levels 2–3). At Levels 4–5, the vision is of a finance function where AI could autonomously manage large parts of the investment portfolio (within human-defined ethical and risk parameters), optimise global cash flow in real-time across different currencies and jurisdictions, and conduct continuous, intelligent auditing of all transactions, with human experts focusing on complex financial strategy, interpreting novel regulatory changes, and providing ultimate ethical oversight.
- **Marketing and Sales:** This function shifts from human-led campaign creation and traditional, relationship-based sales processes (Levels 0–1) to a world of AI-driven customer segmentation, personalised marketing automation, predictive lead scoring, and AI-powered chatbots for initial customer interactions (Levels 2–3). At Levels 4–5, marketing could become a hyper-personalised, dynamically adaptive conversation co-created with AI, which continuously analyses customer data and market responses to optimise every interaction. AI agents might handle significant parts of the sales cycle for standard products, with human sales professionals focusing their efforts on high-value strategic relationships, complex enterprise-level negotiations, and acting as ethical brand ambassadors.
- **Operations and Production:** This is often where the impact of autonomy is most visible. The function moves from manual labour and human-controlled machinery with linear planning (Levels 0–1) towards the reality of smart factories with integrated IoT sensors, predictive maintenance, widespread robotic automation,

and AI-optimised supply chains (Levels 2–3). At Levels 4–5, the vision is of highly autonomous, self-configuring, and self-healing production systems and supply networks, with humans taking on roles of system design, strategic network orchestration, resilience planning (e.g. how to reconfigure the network in response to a geopolitical shock), and providing ethical oversight of resource use and environmental impact.

– **Research and Development (R&D):** The R&D function transforms from being a process of human-led, often intuition-driven discovery and manual experimentation (Levels 0–1) to one where AI assists in analysing vast research literature and simulation tools accelerate testing (Levels 2–3). At Levels 4–5, as discussed earlier, AI becomes a true research partner, capable of generating novel hypotheses, designing complex experiments, and analysing massive datasets to accelerate discovery in fields like materials science, drug development, and climate modelling, with human scientists providing creative direction, critical validation, ethical oversight, and translating abstract discoveries into real-world applications.

New Roles, Fading Roles: Negotiating the Workforce Transition

The progression towards SDOs inevitably means that some traditional job roles, particularly those characterised by repetitive, predictable, and data-intensive tasks, will diminish or disappear. This reality, however, does not necessarily imply net job destruction, but it does require a workforce transformation and role evolution that will be one of the most significant social and economic shifts of the twenty-first century (Autor, 2015). Roles that are heavily focused on high-volume data entry, routine report generation, and rule-based customer service are most susceptible to substitution. Yet, this displacement creates the space for a host of new and evolved roles to emerge. This transition demands proactive adaptation from individuals, organisations, and society as a whole. What follows is a field guide to some of the critical human roles that will define the SDO workforce.

– **AI/Data Specialists:** This category represents the technical core of the SDO, responsible for building and maintaining its cognitive engine. The demand for these roles will grow exponentially, but it will also become more specialised. Beyond generalist data scientists, SDOs will require machine learning engineers who productionise and scale models reliably; AI trainers and data curators who meticulously clean, label, and manage the vast datasets required for training, ensuring data quality and mitigating bias at the source; and AI system auditors who can rigorously test and validate the performance, safety, and fairness of AI models.

– **Human-Machine Interaction (HMI/HXI) Designers:** As work becomes a partnership between people and algorithms, a new breed of professional is needed to architect that collaboration. HMI/HXI designers are the user-experience experts for the autonomous age. They go far beyond designing dashboards. Their job is to deeply understand the context in which human-AI collaboration occurs – from the factory floor to the boardroom – and to design interfaces and workflows that are intuitive, effective, and build trust. They conduct research with employees to understand friction points and use techniques from cognitive science and design thinking to ensure the AI's output is not just accurate, but also explainable and actionable for its human partners.

- **Process Automation and Orchestration Specialists:** These individuals are the master plumbers and civil engineers of the SDO. They analyse, design, and manage the complex, automated workflows that form the organisation's operational backbone. Possessing a hybrid skillset of deep process knowledge (akin to a Lean Six Sigma black belt) and technical expertise in RPA, IA, and API integrations, they identify bottlenecks in legacy processes and re-engineer them for an autonomous world. They ensure the seamless flow of data and decisions between different systems, connecting the AI brain to the automated limbs of the organisation.

- **Strategic Advisors and Complex Problem Solvers:** As AI handles more of the routine analytical work, the value of deep human expertise combined with advanced critical thinking will soar. These roles are for the individuals who can take the insights generated by AI and apply creativity, systems thinking, and contextual knowledge to solve novel, unstructured, and ambiguous problems. They are the leaders who will navigate a "black swan" event, the strategists who can devise a competitive strategy in a new market where no data exists, and the scientists who can form a new hypothesis based on a surprising correlation uncovered by a machine.

- **Ethical Governance and Compliance Experts for AI:** An SDO cannot operate without a strong moral compass and a robust framework for risk management. This creates a critical need for professionals who can ensure autonomous systems operate responsibly, fairly, and legally. These are not traditional compliance officers. They are specialists who understand the intricacies of algorithmic bias, data privacy, and AI safety. They work with legal teams to navigate regulations like GDPR, with HR to audit hiring algorithms for fairness, and with development teams to conduct "Ethical Impact Assessments" *before* a new AI system is deployed, embedding ethical considerations into the design process from day one.

- **"New Collar" Workers:** This term describes a vital and growing category of the workforce that bridges the gap between traditional blue-collar and white-collar roles. These are hands-on technical jobs that require specialised skills but not necessarily a traditional university degree. These skills are often acquired through focused vocational training, apprenticeships, or industry certifications. Examples include the robotics technician who maintains and troubleshoots the fleet of autonomous robots in a warehouse, the smart factory operator who supervises and fine-tunes AI-driven machinery, or the drone fleet manager for an autonomous logistics network.

- **Roles Emphasising Uniquely Human Skills:** As autonomy absorbs predictable tasks, the economic value and societal importance of capabilities that are uniquely human will increase dramatically. Jobs that are fundamentally centred on empathy, complex interpersonal communication, compassionate care, creative arts, and high-stakes, detailed negotiation will not only persist but will become premium roles. An AI can analyse a patient's medical data, but it cannot provide the compassionate care of a nurse. An AI can generate marketing copy, but it cannot match the vision of a creative director or the ethical leadership of a CEO. In the world of the SDO, our most human skills become our most valuable assets (Roose, 2022).

"Progressive Autonomy": A Responsible and Managed Path Forward

The transition towards higher levels of organisational autonomy, with its implications for the workforce, necessitates a responsible and managed approach. The concept of "progressive autonomy" offers a valuable framework for this. It suggests a staged, deliberate, and human-centric transition from predominantly human-led operations and governance towards more algorithmically managed and autonomous systems. This implies a societal and organisational commitment to several key principles:

- **Investing Heavily in Reskilling and Upskilling:** Organisations, educational institutions, and governments have a collective responsibility to help the workforce adapt. This means providing accessible and effective training in new technologies, data literacy, digital skills, critical thinking, ethical reasoning, and other competencies that complement AI and enable individuals to transition into new or evolved roles.
- **Focusing on Augmentation, Not Replacement:** Framing automation and AI primarily as tools to *augment* human capabilities, rather than solely as means of replacement. The strategic goal should be to free people from drudgery, routine, and hazardous tasks, allowing them to focus on more engaging, creative, strategic, and intrinsically human work that values their unique strengths.
- **Proactive Change Management and Transparent Communication:** Organisations must be transparent with their employees about the strategic direction regarding automation and autonomy, the anticipated changes to roles and processes, and the support that will be available during the transition. Involving employees in the design and implementation of new systems where feasible can foster buy-in, reduce fear and resistance, and lead to better outcomes.
- **Prioritising Ethical Considerations and Fairness:** Proactively addressing the ethical implications of job displacement and ensuring fairness and equity in how automation is implemented are paramount. This includes considering the differential impact of automation on various groups of workers and developing strategies to mitigate negative consequences and ensure that the benefits of increased productivity are shared broadly.

The self-driving organisation, when designed and implemented thoughtfully and ethically, is not always an entity that is antithetical or hostile to human potential. Instead, it can be an organisation where humans and machines operate in a powerful partnership (Orlikowski, 1992). The ultimate goal should be to create organisations that are not only more efficient, agile, and resilient but also more human-focused environments that allow people to contribute their unique talents in more meaningful, fulfilling, and beneficial ways.

Key Takeaways

- **The Future of Work Is a Partnership:** Increasing organisational autonomy leads to a sophisticated partnership between people and machines. This creates a whole that is far greater than the sum of its parts by strategically allocating work to create human-machine collaboration and augmentation.
- **The Paradox of Humanity:** The most effective path to a more human-centric workplace, one that leverages our unique talents for creativity and empathy relies directly on advanced autonomy.
- **Leveraging Complementary Strengths:** The optimal allocation of work is based on understanding the complementary strengths of humans and machines.
    - *Humans* excel in domains requiring creativity, complex critical thinking, empathy, ethical judgement, and adaptability to true novelty.
    - *Machines* are unparalleled in tasks that demand speed, scale, consistency, high-volume data processing, pattern recognition, and optimisation.
- **The Evolving Division of Labour Across the SOA:** The roles of humans and machines are reconfigured at each level of the spectrum:
    - At lower levels (0–2), humans perform most tasks, with technology augmenting their abilities or automating simple, discrete functions.
    - At mid-levels (3), the balance shifts significantly, with machines autonomously managing complex processes and humans transitioning to higher-level oversight and exception handling.
    - At higher levels (4), work becomes a true symbiotic partnership, where humans and AI co-create value by collaborating on complex problems.
- **Workforce Transformation Creates New Roles:** The journey towards autonomy will diminish roles focused on repetitive tasks while simultaneously creating a host of new and evolved roles. These include AI/Data Specialists, Human-Machine Interaction (HMI) Designers, AI Ethicists, and a vital category of "New Collar" Workers with specialised technical skills.
- **"Progressive Autonomy" as a Responsible Path Forward:** This book advocates for a deliberate, managed, and human-centric approach to this transition. This framework involves a societal and organisational commitment to heavily investing in reskilling the workforce, focusing on augmenting human capabilities, and prioritising fairness and transparent communication.

Chapter 6
Social Codes: Legal, Compliance, and Security

On a rain-slicked motorway in the early hours of the morning, blue flashing lights of emergency vehicles illuminate the wreckage of a multi-car pile-up. An investigator in a high-visibility jacket surveys the scene. The initial cause seems clear: one car, a high-end electric sedan, swerved suddenly across three lanes, triggering the chain reaction. The driver, however, stands by the side of the road, shaken but insistent. His hands were on his lap; the car was driving itself.

The investigation shifts from the driver to the vehicle's manufacturer. In a conference room a week later, a team of lawyers gathers. They are faced with a legal puzzle that has no precedent. The car's logs show its sensors correctly identified a large object tumbling from the truck ahead. The AI, executing its programmed ethical framework, had milliseconds to make a choice: collide with the object, swerve left into oncoming traffic, or swerve right into the concrete barrier. It chose the barrier, an action that saved its occupant but initiated the wider crash.

There was no human negligence in the traditional sense. There was only the car's decision, an outcome of millions of lines of code written by hundreds of programmers and trained on petabytes of simulation data. Who is liable for the damages? The owner who activated the system? The programmers who wrote the decision-making code? The company that marketed the car as "autonomous"?

This scenario illustrates the collision of twenty-first-century technology with twentieth-century law. As organisations become more autonomous, they venture into a world where the established social codes – the legal, compliance, and security frameworks that govern corporate conduct – are becoming dangerously outdated. This chapter explores this new, high-stakes landscape, examining the rules of the road for an age when the driver is no longer human.

Overview

As organisations accelerate their journey towards autonomy, they venture into a world where the established Social Codes – the legal, compliance, and security frameworks that govern corporate conduct – are no longer adequate to govern autonomous conduct. This chapter confronts this critical challenge, exploring how the very "rules of the road" are being fractured and rewritten by the advent of AI-driven decisions and decentralised architectures. The issues examined here are not peripheral concerns; they are central to an SDO's viability, trustworthiness, and its fundamental social licence to operate.

Our analysis begins with the evolving legal and compliance landscape, charting a course from the familiar terrain of human-centric law into the terra incognita of algorithmic accountability. We dissect the challenges to traditional concepts of liability, from assigning responsibility when an autonomous system causes harm to the ambiguous legal status of entities like DAOs, which operate beyond conventional jurisdictions.

Next, we map the fundamentally reshaped cybersecurity threat landscape. The chapter moves beyond traditional IT security to identify the novel attack surfaces created by autonomy itself, including the risks of data poisoning, adversarial attacks on AI models, and the exploitation of smart contract vulnerabilities. To counter these threats, we will explore how modern operational practices like DevSecOps and Chaos Engineering are becoming essential guardrails for building resilient systems. By the end of this chapter, you will understand the new categories of risk inherent in the autonomous age and the proactive strategies required to navigate them, ensuring that innovation proceeds on a secure and legally sound foundation.

Introduction

As organisations accelerate their journey across the Spectrum of Organisational Autonomy (SOA), they are navigating novel technological frontiers while simultaneously entering an increasingly complex, often ambiguous, and rapidly evolving legal, compliance, and security landscape. The established "rules of the road" that have governed traditional business conduct – developed over decades, sometimes centuries, of precedent, legislation, and practice – are being stretched beyond their limits, reinterpreted, or found entirely inadequate in the face of AI-driven decision-making, decentralised organisational architectures, the exponential proliferation of data powering these self-driving entities, and the sheer velocity at which they operate.

The very concepts of liability, accountability, due diligence, and intellectual property are being called into question (Calo, 2015). When an algorithm makes a decision that causes harm, who is responsible? When a decentralised organisation with no legal address or appointed leaders facilitates a transaction, which jurisdiction's laws apply? And how can an organisation defend itself against a new breed of cybersecurity threats that target the very cognitive engines of its autonomous operations? This chapter meticulously examines these critical challenges, exploring how the legal and compliance landscape shifts across the SOA, what new and amplified security threats emerge, and how organisations can strategically build resilience, while adhering to legal mandates and safeguarding themselves against novel breeds of risk. This is not a matter of peripheral concern; it is central to the viability, trustworthiness, and social license to operate for any aspiring SDO.

The Evolving Legal and Compliance Landscape: From Established Precedents to Terra Incognita

The progression across the SOA is inevitably also a journey into increasingly intricate and often uncharted legal and compliance terrain. What is relatively well-defined and understood at lower levels of autonomy becomes progressively ambiguous, contentious, and subject to reinterpretation at higher levels, pushing existing legal frameworks to new limits and beyond.

At Level 0, the legal and compliance landscape is largely familiar terrain. The core areas of concern revolve around well-established legal doctrines. Employment law governs the relationship with the human workforce. Contract law provides the framework for agreements with suppliers and customers. Product liability law assigns responsibility for faulty goods. Tort law, particularly the concept of negligence, establishes accountability when an organisation's actions (or inactions) cause harm to others. In this world, lines of accountability are generally clear. If a faulty product injures a consumer, liability can be traced through a human-managed design process, human-supervised manufacturing lines, and human-led quality control. If the company makes a fraudulent financial statement, accountability can be assigned to the human executives who signed off on it. The legal system is built around the presumption of human agency and intent.

The journey into complexity begins at Level 1, as AI tools begin to assist human decision-making. Here, the first ripples of new legal challenges appear, particularly in the areas of discrimination and intellectual property. If an organisation uses an AI tool to help screen job candidates or assess creditworthiness, and that tool was trained on historical data reflecting societal biases, it may inadvertently recommend biased outcomes. Even if a human makes the final decision, if they are consistently relying on biased recommendations, the organisation could face significant legal challenges related to discrimination. Proving that the human decision was truly independent of the biased AI input becomes a difficult legal hurdle. Similarly, questions arise regarding the intellectual property (IP) of AI-assisted creations. If a designer uses a generative AI tool to help create a new logo, who is the "author" in the eyes of copyright law? Is it the human designer, the developer of the AI tool, or is the output even eligible for copyright protection at all? Data privacy regulations like the EU's General Data Protection Regulation (GDPR) and California's Consumer Privacy Act (CCPA) also come into sharper focus, as the AI's use of personal data must be transparent, justified, and compliant with principles like the "right to explanation."(Price and Cohen, 2021).

At Level 2, with specific tasks handled autonomously under human oversight, questions of accountability for automated actions become significantly more involved. The chain of causation is no longer simple. If an automated workflow for processing insurance claims, governed by rules configured by a business team, wrongly denies a valid claim, leading to financial harm for the claimant, determining the precise locus of responsibility becomes a complex legal puzzle. Is it the human team that oversaw the system but may have been suffering from automation complacency? Is it the individuals who initially configured the rules but failed to anticipate this specific edge case? Or could there be product liability associated with the design of the automation tool itself, if it lacked adequate safeguards or transparency features? The legal principle of "reasonable foreseeability" becomes difficult to apply when dealing with the emergent behaviour of complex automated systems.

The landscape shifts into truly challenging territory at Level 3 where AI systems make significant operational decisions autonomously within their defined domains. This is where existing legal frameworks begin to fracture. The classic example is the autonomous vehicle (AV). If an AV operating at this level is involved in an accident-causing injury, determining who is legally liable becomes a central and fiercely debated legal question. Is it the owner, who may not have been driving? Is it the software programmers who wrote the millions of lines of decision-making code? Is it the manufacturer who assembled the vehicle and its sensors? Is it the provider of the mapping data the AV relied upon? Traditional tort law, based on proving a human driver's negligence, is ill-suited to this scenario. Courts and legislators are grappling with whether to apply strict product liability standards to the manufacturer or to develop entirely new legal frameworks for autonomous systems. The "black box" nature of some sophisticated AI models – where even their creators cannot fully explain the reasoning behind a specific output – poses a challenge to the legal process of discovery, where parties must be able to examine the evidence and logic behind a decision. This has made the development of explainable AI an important technical goal and a legal necessity (Adadi and Berrada, 2018; Gunning and Aha, 2019). Furthermore, the enforceability of smart contracts, which can operate at this level, comes under pressure. If a smart contract has a bug that leads to an unintended and unfair outcome, how can the dispute be resolved when "code is law" and there is no traditional legal text to interpret or court to appeal to?

At Level 4, the legal context becomes exceptionally complex, almost a different world. For example, as mentioned in Chapter 3, the legal status of DAOs, a potential archetype for Level 4 entities, is still a disputed issue globally. In most jurisdictions, DAOs lack clear legal personality. This means they are not recognised as distinct legal entities like corporations or partnerships. The default legal treatment in many common law systems may be to consider them as "general partnerships." This has a potentially chilling consequence for their members: each participant could be subject to "joint and several liability," meaning they are all personally, and potentially unlimitedly, liable for the entirety of the DAO's debts and legal infringements, even those resulting from actions taken by other anonymous members. This single issue is a massive deterrent to mainstream participation and a critical barrier to the growth of DAOs. While jurisdictions like Wyoming in the USA have passed specific legislation to recognise DAOs as a specific form of legal entity (the DAO LLC), this is far from a global standard. This lack of legal clarity creates ambiguity regarding a DAO's ability to own property, enter into enforceable contracts with traditional entities, or pay taxes. Jurisdictional ambiguity is another immense hurdle. For a global DAO with anonymous members in dozens of countries, whose laws apply. How can regulations be enforced? The complex taxation of crypto-assets and the transactions executed by these entities further complicates the already complex compliance picture. Finally, IP ownership in the context of human-AI co-creation, a hallmark of Level 4, becomes a tangled legal frontier, challenging the very definition of inventorship and authorship in patent and copyright law.

In the theoretical realm of Level 5, our existing legal and compliance frameworks are entirely inadequate. They are based on a world of human actors, human accountability, and human-controlled tools. This stage would necessitate a fundamental rethinking of foundational legal concepts. Would a truly autonomous, self-evolving AI require some form of legal personhood (Chopra and White, 2011), similar to corporate personhood, to operate in the world? If so, what rights and, more importantly, what responsibilities would it have? Could it be held accountable for its actions? The "control problem" for superintelligent AI, a central concern in AI safety research, becomes the ultimate legal and compliance challenge: how might we regulate, constrain, and hold accountable an entity that may be intellectually able to outmanoeuvre its creators?

Cybersecurity in an Increasingly Autonomous World: New Threats, Amplified Defences

In addition to creating legal complexity, the transition to SDOs fundamentally reshapes the cybersecurity landscape, demanding a shift in thinking from traditional perimeter defence to a model of deep, systemic resilience. The same technologies that enable autonomy – interconnected systems, vast data reservoirs, and complex AI models – also create novel attack surfaces and magnify the potential consequences of a breach. In an SDO, a security failure transcends being an IT problem to become an existential threat that can lead to catastrophic operational failures, massive financial loss, or even direct physical harm.

The new risks begin at the level of the code itself, particularly with the smart contract vulnerabilities that are most prominent at Levels 3 and 4. As the infamous 2016 hack of "The DAO" demonstrated and described in Chapter 3, flaws in the code of smart contracts can be ruthlessly exploited by malicious actors to drain funds or manipulate governance. Because blockchain transactions are immutable, these hacks are often irreversible, making the financial finality of the code both a feature and a critical vulnerability. Common exploits go beyond the "re-entrancy" attack that doomed the DAO – where an attacker effectively tricks a contract into giving them money repeatedly before it can update its own balance – and include subtle issues like integer overflows and timestamp dependencies. Defence against these threats requires a multi-layered, hyper-diligent approach. This includes rigorous independent security audits of all code before deployment, the use of formal verification techniques to mathematically prove the correctness of the code's logic, generous "bug bounty" programmes to incentivise "white-hat" hackers to find flaws before malicious actors do, and adherence to secure coding best practices developed by the community.

Beyond the contract code, the AI models at the heart of an SDO are themselves prime targets for a new class of novel attacks that target the system's "mind." Data poisoning, for instance, involves secretly corrupting the training data used to build a model, subtly teaching it a malicious or unpredictable behaviour that only manifests once it is deployed. Another sophisticated threat comes from adversarial attacks, which involve tricking a model with subtly altered inputs that are often imperceptible to humans but cause the AI to make a gross misclassification. An attacker could change a few pixels in an image to make a self-driving car's vision system mistake a stop sign for a speed limit sign or alter an audio file in a way that is inaudible to a person but causes a voice-activated system to execute a dangerous command. Other threats include model stealing, which is the reverse engineering of a proprietary model to steal valuable intellectual property, and membership inference attacks, which can determine if a specific individual's data was used in the training set, a major privacy concern. Defending the cognitive engine of the SDO involves robust data validation and sanitation, a technique known as adversarial training to make models more robust by exposing them to these attacks in a controlled environment, the use of differential privacy techniques to protect individual data, and model encryption.

These specific threats are layered on top of the monumental challenge of data security and privacy at scale. SDOs run on vast quantities of data about customers, operations, and employees which is both a hugely valuable asset and a massive liability if breached. Protecting this data from exfiltration by external attackers or misuse by insiders requires a "defence-in-depth" strategy. This includes end-to-end encryption for data at rest and in transit, strong access controls based on the principle of least privilege, regular vulnerability assessments and penetration testing, and a corporate culture that adheres to privacy-by-design principles, where privacy considerations are embedded in the design of every system from the outset.

As autonomy moves into the physical world, new vectors of attack emerge that can bridge the digital and physical realms. The proliferation of interconnected IoT devices – the billions of sensors and actuators that form the SDO's interface with the physical world – creates millions of potential entry points for attackers. A compromised sensor in a smart factory could feed false data into an AI system, leading to incorrect decisions with direct physical consequences, such as causing a machine to operate in an unsafe manner or ruining an entire batch of product. A hacked fleet of delivery drones could be turned into a botnet or directed to a single location, causing chaos. Similarly, the physical security of autonomous systems is critical, as robots, drones, and vehicles can be subject to physical tampering, theft, or vandalism that could compromise their function or safety. Defence in this domain involves secure device provisioning and authentication, a strategy for regular and automated firmware updates, network segmentation to isolate critical devices, and tamper-evident hardware.

Finally, the human element presents its own complex risk. A malicious or simply negligent action by an employee with legitimate access to a critical system can cause significant damage. As systems become more powerful, the potential damage from a single insider action increases. The standard defence involves robust monitoring of user activity for anomalous behaviour. However, this creates a surveillance dilemma for the culture. These same powerful monitoring tools can be repurposed for pervasive internal surveillance, creating a culture of distrust that undermines the psychological safety required for innovation. When employees feel they are under constant digital observation, the organisation risks becoming a form of panopticon, where the fear of being monitored stifles the very creativity and open communication that an SDO is meant to foster. Defence, therefore, requires a careful balance: enforcing the principle of least privilege and monitoring for anomalies, while also being transparent with employees about what is being monitored and why, to preserve the trust that is the foundation of a collaborative and resilient culture.

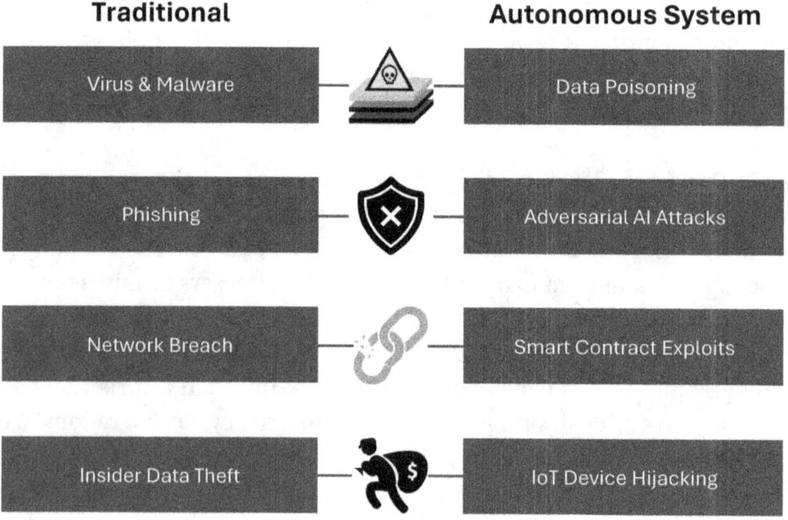

Figure 6: The evolving cybersecurity threat landscape across the Spectrum of Organisational Autonomy.

Building Resilience: Modern Operational Practices as Guardrails

In the face of these escalating legal and security risks, a reactive posture is insufficient. Leading organisations are adopting a suite of modern operational philosophies and practices to build systems that are secure, compliant, and resilient by design.

These practices represent a cultural shift towards continuous improvement, shared responsibility, and a proactive approach to managing risk.

This begins with the cultural and professional movement of DevOps, which emphasises collaboration and automation to enable faster, more reliable software updates. Its evolution, DevSecOps, integrates security into every phase of this life cycle. By "shifting security left," security becomes a shared responsibility of the development and operations teams from the very beginning. Instead of being a final, often rushed, check at the end of the process, automated security testing is built directly into the development pipeline, ensuring that systems are built with a secure foundation from their inception.

This philosophy is implemented with technical rigor through the practice of GitOps. This approach uses a distributed version control system like Git as the single source of truth for declaratively managing both application code and infrastructure configuration. The mindset shifts from an imperative one, where an engineer manually logs in to a server to make a change, to a declarative one, where the desired state of the system is defined in a configuration file. That file is then reviewed, approved, and tracked in Git, and an automated process ensures the live environment converges to that desired state. This provides an immutable, auditable log of every change made to the system, which is invaluable for both security forensics and legal discovery.

In a complex SDO with dozens of interacting microservices and AI models, it becomes difficult to predict every failure mode. This is where observability extends beyond traditional monitoring. While monitoring tells you if a system you already understand is broken, observability is about designing systems that provide the data needed to understand failures you could never predict. It involves designing systems that emit rich, detailed telemetry through a combination of logs, metrics, and traces. This allows teams to quickly understand, diagnose, and resolve novel issues in these complex autonomous systems by asking new questions of the data, rather than relying on pre-defined dashboards.

To build confidence in a system's ability to withstand turbulent conditions, leaders can champion chaos engineering. This is the disciplined, experimental practice of proactively and intentionally injecting controlled failures into systems – simulating server outages, network latency, or API failures. The goal is to identify weaknesses and build more fault-tolerant, antifragile systems before real-world failures cause disruption. It is a disciplined, experimental approach to building confidence, moving resilience from a theoretical assumption to a tested and proven capability.

These same principles of discipline and automation are then applied to the cognitive core of the SDO through DataOps and MLOps. These are specialised disciplines that apply agile and DevOps principles to the life cycles of data analytics and machine learning. An AI model can fail not just because of a bug in its code, but because the real-world data it receives has changed in subtle ways, a phenomenon known as "data drift." MLOps aims to automate the entire ML pipeline, from data ingestion and model training to deployment, and importantly, continuous monitoring in production.

This improves the quality, reliability, and security of the data and AI that power the organisation, ensuring its cognitive components are robust and dependable.

The Urgent Need for Agile and Adaptive Policymaking

The challenges outlined in this chapter cannot be solved by organisations alone. There is a pressing need for a parallel evolution in our legal and regulatory frameworks. The traditional "pacing problem" – where technology evolves much faster than law can keep up – is more acute than ever. Traditional regulatory toolkits, often based on writing slow-moving, prescriptive rules, are ill-suited for the rapid and unpredictable pace of SDO development.

Policymakers must therefore embrace more agile and adaptive approaches to governance (Yeung, 2018). This includes the use of regulatory sandboxes, which allow firms to test innovative new products, services, and business models in a controlled environment under regulatory supervision. It involves a shift towards outcome-based regulation, which focuses on the results an organisation achieves (e.g. maintaining a certain level of system safety or data privacy) rather than prescribing the specific technology or process they must use. It requires new forms of collaboration between regulators and industry, and a concerted effort to establish legal clarity and certainty for novel entities like DAOs. Creating this legal and security certainty should not be interpreted as a barrier to innovation; it is a necessary pre-condition and enabler for it. It gives organisations the confidence to invest, experiment, and scale, knowing they

Table 5: Legal and security challenges across the SOA.

Level	Primary legal/compliance challenge	Primary security threat
0/1	Established law (employment, contract, and tort); human liability	Traditional IT security (network and malware)
2	Accountability for automated errors; IP of AI-assisted work	Data integrity for automation; API security
3	Liability for autonomous systems (e.g. AVs); "black box" problem	Data poisoning; adversarial attacks on AI models
4	Ambiguous legal status of DAOs; jurisdictional ambiguity	Smart contract exploits; economic/governance attacks on DAOs
5	The "AI control problem"; creating new legal frameworks for AGI	Security of AGI; ensuring integrity of its core objectives

are operating on solid ground. Ultimately, the goal must be to foster an enabling environment for responsible innovation that diligently safeguards the public interest and ensures that the immense power of these new organisational forms is aligned with enduring societal values.

Key Takeaways

- **Established "Social Codes" Are Under Strain:** The journey towards autonomy is fracturing the established legal, compliance, and security frameworks that have historically governed business conduct. This creates a new landscape of risk and ambiguity for organisations.
- **The Legal Landscape is Evolving into "Terra Incognita":** As organisations ascend the SOA, legal concepts like liability and accountability become progressively more complex. The lines of responsibility blur for harms caused by autonomous systems, and the legal status of novel entities like DAOs remains a critical, unresolved issue in most jurisdictions.
- **A New Generation of Cybersecurity Threats Has Emerged:** Autonomy creates new and amplified security vulnerabilities. These include risks specific to the core technologies, such as the exploitation of flawed smart contracts, adversarial attacks designed to deceive AI models, and the security weaknesses inherent in vast networks of IoT devices.
- **Modern Operational Practices Are Essential Guardrails:** To navigate these new risks, organisations are adopting modern operational philosophies to build resilience and security directly into their systems. These practices include DevSecOps, which integrates security into the entire software development life cycle, and Chaos Engineering, the proactive practice of testing a system's ability to withstand failure.
- **A Call for Agile and Adaptive Policymaking:** The rapid pace of technological change requires a parallel evolution in our legal and regulatory frameworks. The chapter calls for policymakers to embrace more agile approaches, such as regulatory sandboxes and outcome-based regulation, to foster responsible innovation while safeguarding the public interest.

Chapter 7
Operating and Behaving: Ethics, Accountability, and Social Impact

Maria had spent two years building her catering business from her small apartment kitchen, earning rave reviews and a loyal clientele. Her business plan for a town centre shop was meticulous, her credit score was excellent, and her projections were conservative. She submitted her application for a small business loan through a major bank's new, hyper-efficient online portal.

It was rejected in seven seconds.

There was no explanation, just a single line: "Application does not meet current risk parameters." When she finally reached a loan officer at the bank, he was apologetic but unhelpful. He looked at her file on his screen and saw the same thing she did: a final, system-generated decision. He confessed he had no way of knowing which of the 1,000 data points the algorithm used had triggered the denial. He could only see its conclusion.

What neither Maria nor the loan officer could see was the ghost in the machine. The AI had been trained on 50 years of the bank's lending data. It had learned, with cold statistical precision, that applicants from Maria's historically low-income postcode had a slightly higher default rate. The system, in its search for patterns, had penalised her for her neighbourhood. It judged her not by her own merits, but by the shadow of a statistical past.

This is where the logic of autonomy collides with the principles of fairness, and economic and common sense. An organisation can be perfectly efficient in its operations and yet produce outcomes that are profoundly unjust. As we cede more authority to autonomous systems, we venture beyond the challenges of legal compliance into the more complex and vital terrain of ethics, accountability, and social impact. This chapter explores the moral maze of this new world, examining the character required to operate and behave responsibly in the autonomous age.

Overview

The traverse across the SOA is an ethical one. This chapter moves beyond legal compliance to explore the moral maze of operating and behaving, confronting the critical questions of fairness, accountability, and societal impact that arise when we cede significant control to autonomous systems. In the autonomous age, ethical integrity is not a public relations exercise but a core component of strategy, risk management, and sustainable competitive advantage.

Our exploration begins with the most immediate and pervasive source of ethical failure associated with AI: algorithmic bias. We dissect how systems can learn and amplify historical prejudices, leading to discriminatory outcomes in critical areas like hiring and lending. We then confront the accountability vacuum – the "problem of many hands" that makes it so difficult to assign responsibility when a complex autonomous system errs – and examine the "black box" problem, where opaque AI models erode trust and hinder our ability to diagnose these failures.

The chapter then broadens its scope to address two forward-looking societal challenges: the ethical obligation to manage job displacement with justice and equity, and the ultimate AI control problem – the challenge of ensuring that highly advanced systems remain aligned with human values. Finally, we will outline the essential components of a robust ethical framework for any SDO, from establishing clear principles to fostering a culture of responsibility. By the end of this chapter, you will understand that building a "wise" organisation is more important than just building a "smart" one.

The Paradox of Intelligence: Building the Wise Organisation

As we progressively cede decision-making authority and operational control from human hands to autonomous systems and decentralised structures, critical questions regarding responsibility, fairness, transparency, and the broader societal consequences of these powerful new organisational forms move from the periphery to the very centre of strategic and public discourse. This traverse across the SOA is, therefore, a journey into increasingly challenging ethical terrain, where the character of an organisation is defined both by what it can do and what it ought to do. While a smart system can optimise a process with incredible efficiency, a wise organisation applies ethical principles and contextual judgement to ensure that its actions are fair, just, and beneficial (Smith, 2019). This fundamental tension between intelligence and wisdom is the key to understanding the specific ethical challenges of algorithmic bias, the accountability vacuum, and the responsible use of influence that we will now explore.

This chapter begins to explore the most prominent aspects of this ethical maze. It highlights the key moral questions, the potential for unintended harms, the systemic challenges to establishing clear accountability, and the overarching priority for a robust, adaptive moral compass to guide the design, development, deployment, and governance of these transformative entities. We move beyond the "what" and "how" of technology to the far more important questions of "should" and "why." The issues discussed here are not abstract philosophical concerns; they are tangible risks that can manifest as catastrophic brand damage, crippling legal liability, the irreversible loss of public trust, and significant, lasting societal harm. For the leaders of aspiring SDOs, ethics should not boil down to tech-washing, a compliance checkbox or a cynical public relations exercise; it is a core component of strategy, risk management, and long-term viability. In the autonomous age, ethical integrity will be a key differentiator and a primary source of legitimacy and sustainable competitive advantage.

At its core, the overarching ethical challenge that this chapter addresses is this: how do we ensure that autonomous organisations, increasingly empowered to make decisions and act independently in the world, operate in alignment with fundamental human values, respect individual rights and dignity, promote justice and equity, and contribute positively to the overall well-being of society?

The Weight of Code: Algorithmic Bias and Its Pervasive Consequences

One of the most pressing and widely discussed ethical challenges in the era of AI and autonomous systems is algorithmic bias (O'Neil, 2016). The problem arises from a simple but powerful truth: AI systems, particularly those based on machine learning, learn from the data they are fed. They are, in essence, pattern-recognition engines. If the data used to train them reflects the historical biases, societal prejudices, or systemic inequalities that are woven into the fabric of our world – whether related to race, gender, age, socioeconomic status, geographical location, or any other characteristic – the AI will inevitably learn, internalise, and in many cases, perpetuate or even amplify those biases in its subsequent decisions and actions. An algorithm, devoid of moral understanding, simply optimises for the patterns it is shown. If the most consistent pattern for a "successful loan applicant" in the historical data is a person from a wealthy neighbourhood, the AI will learn that pattern. It does not understand the underlying socioeconomic forces; it only sees the correlation.

Bias can be encoded in subtle ways. It can arise from unrepresentative training data, where certain demographic groups are underrepresented, leading the AI to perform poorly for those groups. It can also arise from proxy variables, where an ostensibly neutral data point, like a person's zip code, serves as a stand-in for a protected characteristic like race, leading to discriminatory outcomes like insurance redlining. The most insidious form is the feedback loop, where a biased prediction (e.g. an AI flagging a certain neighbourhood for heavier policing) leads to actions (more arrests in that area) that generate new data confirming the original bias, creating a vicious, self-reinforcing cycle of discrimination (Eubanks, 2018).

The manifestation and impact of algorithmic bias grow more severe as an organisation traverses the SOA, with the ethical risks scaling in proportion to the autonomy of the system. This is a journey from rectifying individual human errors to confronting systemic, automated injustice.

At **Level 0**, in a human-centric organisation, the primary ethical concern is traditional human bias in decision-making. This includes the full range of cognitive biases – confirmation bias, affinity bias, stereotyping – that can lead to unfair outcomes. Even at this stage, the uncritical use of simple algorithms or statistical models, such as using historical sales data to predict performance, can begin to codify these unexamined human biases into seemingly objective formal processes, laying a foundation for more significant issues later on.

The risks become more tangible and insidious at **Level 1**, assisted autonomy, where algorithmic bias can subtly influence the AI tools used to assist human decision-makers, creating a powerful "bias-in, bias-out" loop. An AI tool used for screening job candidates, for example, might learn from 20 years of a company's hiring data that most successful executives were male. It might then learn to correlate male-associated keywords, like "captain" of a sports team, or even names on a resume with a higher chance of success, systematically down-ranking equally qualified female candidates (Dastin, 2018). The danger here is compounded by automation bias – the tendency for humans to place a high degree of trust in an automated system. A human recruiter, presented with a biased shortlist generated by a system perceived as "objective," may then perpetuate this discrimination under a veneer of data-driven neutrality, creating a legally and ethically toxic hiring process that is harder to challenge than one based on overt human prejudice.

As an organisation reaches **Levels 2 and 3**, where AI takes on more direct decision-making authority within defined parameters, the impact of embedded bias becomes more severe, systemic, and harder to detect or override. The scale and speed of automated decisions mean that a single biased rule can affect thousands of people before it is discovered. Consider an AI used for automated parole recommendations, which learns from historical data that individuals from a certain zip code have a higher recidivism rate. The AI may recommend denying parole to a candidate from that area, acting on the statistical correlation while being unable to account for the complex socioeconomic factors that contribute to that statistic or the individual's specific circumstances. Similarly, an AI-driven dynamic pricing model for car insurance might charge higher premiums in minority neighbourhoods, acting on the historical data that correlates those neighbourhoods with higher claim rates, independent of individual driving records. In these cases, the AI is simply executing its programmed logic on biased data, leading to demonstrably unfair treatment and life-altering negative consequences, often without a clear and accessible process for appeal.

At the advanced stages of **Levels 4 and 5**, in highly autonomous systems making complex decisions across broad societal domains, unmitigated algorithmic biases could lead to large-scale, deeply entrenched, and difficult-to-detect discrimination. The issue evolves from biased individual decisions to the risk of creating self-reinforcing feedback loops that shape society itself. An autonomous urban planning AI, learning from historical data, could consistently allocate fewer resources for parks and public transport to poorer neighbourhoods, which in turn could lead to worse health and economic outcomes in those areas, generating new data that "justifies" the initial biased allocation. A fully autonomous content moderation system could systematically silence the voices of minority groups if its training data fails to adequately represent their dialects or cultural norms, effectively shaping public discourse. At this scale, the potential for societal harm becomes immense, as the bias is no longer just an error in the system, but a structural feature of the autonomous world it helps to create (Noble, 2018).

Addressing algorithmic bias requires a multi-pronged, socio-technical approach that must be woven into the fabric of the organisation. This is a continuous process of diligence, involving interventions at the level of data, algorithms, and, most importantly, human culture and oversight. It requires moving beyond a compliance mindset to one of active ethical stewardship.

The work begins with the foundation of any AI system: its data. A commitment to robust data governance and preprocessing involves meticulously auditing training datasets to identify and mitigate historical biases before they ever reach the model. This means looking for sampling biases, where certain groups are underrepresented, and historical biases, where the data reflects past societal prejudices. This can include techniques like resampling or reweighting data to ensure fair representation of different demographic groups, or even algorithmically altering data to remove correlations with protected characteristics. This is a critical, foundational step, as any bias that enters the model at this stage will be amplified by the system's logic.

From the data, attention turns to the algorithms themselves. A proactive approach involves developing and utilising machine learning algorithms specifically designed to promote fairness. Computer scientists have developed various mathematical definitions of fairness – such as "demographic parity," which ensures outcomes are similar across groups, or "equalised odds," which ensures the error rates are similar across groups. These principles can be built into the model's objective function. This often involves a conscious trade-off, as optimising for a specific fairness metric may come at a slight cost to raw predictive accuracy. This is a decision with its own ethical weight that requires a conscious strategic choice, forcing the organisation to define what it values most.

Once a model is built, it must be subject to rigorous bias audits and testing. This is a continuous process, not a one-time check. Organisations must regularly and rigorously test their AI models for biased outcomes against different demographic groups, both before deployment and after. Post-deployment monitoring is crucial, as new biases can emerge over time as the system interacts with the world and the underlying data patterns shift – a phenomenon known as "model drift." This process of verification is greatly aided by a commitment to transparency and explainable AI. Developing and using techniques to understand *why* an AI model is making particular predictions is fundamental for uncovering and diagnosing hidden biases, providing the evidence needed for both internal improvement and external accountability.

Ultimately, technical solutions are only as effective as the people who build and oversee them. Fostering diversity of gender, race, discipline, and life experience within the teams that design, build, and test AI systems is imperative. A homogenous team may have blind spots and fail to consider how a system might impact different communities. A diverse team is more likely to ask the right questions, challenge assumptions, and identify potential biases early in the development process. This extends beyond engineers to include ethicists, social scientists, and domain experts who can provide a more holistic perspective on a system's potential impact.

The final and most critical ethical backstop is the implementation of meaningful human oversight and appeal mechanisms. Especially for high-stakes decisions that significantly impact people's lives, such as in hiring, lending, or justice, there must be a clear, accessible, and effective process for individuals to appeal decisions they believe to be unfair. "Meaningful" oversight means that the human in the loop is empowered with the time, information, context, and authority to genuinely scrutinise and, if necessary, override the system's recommendation. This ensures that the autonomous system remains a tool to assist human judgement, rather than a final, unassailable authority, and that fairness remains a human responsibility.

The Accountability Vacuum: Who Is Responsible When an SDO Errs?

When a traditional organisation makes a mistake that causes harm, lines of accountability, while sometimes complex, generally point towards identifiable human decision-makers or established corporate entities. A CEO can be fired, a board can be held liable, or a specific manager can be held responsible for a negligent decision. Our legal and moral frameworks are built on the concept of human agency (Nissenbaum, 1996). However, in an SDO, especially at higher levels of autonomy, establishing clear responsibility becomes profoundly challenging, creating a dangerous "accountability vacuum."

This problem is often referred to as the "problem of many hands," where a negative outcome is the result of a complex chain of actions by many different people, systems, and organisations, making it difficult to assign blame to any single actor (Matthias, 2004). If an autonomous surgical robot at Level 3 makes a mistake during an operation due to a software error, who is responsible for the patient's injury? Is it the programmers who wrote the millions of lines of code? The hospital that deployed the robot? The surgeon who was supervising but trusted the system? The manufacturer of the robot's hardware or its sensors? The regulator who approved the device for use? Each party can plausibly point to another, diffusing responsibility until it effectively disappears.

This vacuum becomes even more pronounced with Level 4 entities like DAOs. If a DAO, governed by anonymous token holders, loses millions in user funds due to an exploit in its smart contracts, or is used to facilitate illegal transactions, who is legally and morally liable? Is it the anonymous developers who wrote the original code but may have long since left the project? Is it every token holder who voted for a particular action? Is it the entire community of members, who may be scattered across the globe? The very decentralisation that gives DAOs their resilience also makes it incredibly difficult to pinpoint a responsible party that can be held to account.

Mitigating this accountability vacuum is one of the most significant challenges for the future of SDOs. It requires a concerted effort on multiple fronts, moving from high-level principles to concrete, operational practices. The goal is to create a web of responsibility that is as robust and distributed as the autonomous systems it is meant to govern.

The effort begins with the establishment of clear legal and regulatory frameworks. As discussed in the previous chapter, policymakers must develop new legal frameworks for assigning liability for harms caused by autonomous systems, including establishing a clear legal status for novel entities. This external clarity provides the stable ground upon which organisations can build their own robust internal SDO governance. This involves proactively designing governance structures with clear lines of accountability. This goes beyond a simple organisational chart to include the creation of new roles and bodies, such as an "AI Safety Officer" or an "AI Ethics Council," with the authority to scrutinise, question, and even halt the deployment of systems that present unacceptable risks. It also means establishing clear protocols for human intervention, defining precisely when and how a human operator should take control, and maintaining meticulous, tamper-proof audit trails of all decisions made by both humans and AI.

This governance framework must be supported by a deep technical commitment to traceability and auditability by design. Systems must be built from the ground up to be auditable, where every decision made by an AI is logged, along with the data, the parameters, and the version of the model that was used. This creates a clear and immutable record – a "chain of custody" for every algorithmic decision – that can be scrutinised after an incident. This is a direct technical response to the "black box" problem, providing the evidence needed to understand a failure, assign responsibility, and prevent its recurrence. This is a vital component in building trustworthy systems that can withstand both legal and public scrutiny.

Finally, these structural and technical measures are given purpose and direction by the adoption of ethical charters and responsibility principles. By publicly articulating a clear ethical charter, an organisation defines its principles regarding accountability for the actions of its autonomous systems. To be effective, these charters must be more than just public relations documents; they must be operationalised. This means integrating them into the design process for new systems, using them as a guide for strategic decision-making, and embedding them into the performance metrics and incentives for the teams that build and manage these systems. This serves as both a public commitment and an internal guide for decision-making, ensuring that the pursuit of autonomy is always anchored in a foundation of human responsibility.

Insuring the Autonomous Future: A New Frontier for Risk Management

The "accountability vacuum" created by complex autonomous systems is a practical challenge for risk management. When liability is diffuse and the root cause of a failure is buried inside a "black box" algorithm, organisations and their victims need clear avenues for financial recourse. While robust governance and ethical design are the primary solutions, the insurance industry will inevitably play a critical role as a societal shock absorber and a powerful driver of best practices. The transition to SDOs necessitates a reinvention of insurance itself, moving from underwriting predictable human error to pricing the novel risks of intelligent machines.

The core challenge is that the nature of risk is shifting dramatically. For a century, auto insurance was built on vast actuarial tables of human driver behaviour, and commercial liability was based on well-understood industrial processes. In the world of the SDO, this historical data becomes less relevant. The risk is now a flaw in millions of lines of code, or a biased dataset that subtly corrupts an AI's decision-making over time. For an underwriter, pricing this risk is a venture into the unknown. Quantifying the financial risk of an adversarial attack on an AI model or a "re-entrancy" bug in a smart contract requires new expertise and new models.

This shifting landscape is giving rise to a new generation of insurance products designed specifically for the autonomous age. One emerging class is algorithmic liability insurance, designed to cover damages arising directly from a decision made by an AI system. This could range from covering the financial losses caused by an AI-driven trading algorithm that goes haywire, to defending against discrimination lawsuits stemming from a biased hiring algorithm. Such policies will require deep technical due diligence, forcing organisations to prove to their insurers that their AI models are robust, tested, and as fair as possible. In the world of decentralised systems, the hacks of DAOs and DeFi protocols have already spurred a nascent but growing market for smart contract and DeFi insurance. These products offer coverage against the direct financial loss of digital assets due to a demonstrable smart contract vulnerability or economic exploit. These policies are often highly specific, covering certain protocols or types of bugs, and represent a market-based attempt to bring a measure of safety and confidence to these otherwise unregulated financial systems.

Finally, the autonomous vehicle provides the classic example of the need for new liability frameworks, giving rise to dedicated autonomous systems insurance. The model is shifting from personal auto policies to complex commercial product liability policies that may need to cover the vehicle manufacturer, the software developer, the sensor provider, and the fleet operator. The ultimate question of who buys the policy – and is therefore incentivised to ensure safety – remains a subject of intense debate among regulators and insurers.

In this way, the insurance industry will become a primary driver for the adoption of the best practices outlined in this book, rewarding organisations that can demonstrate a mature, resilient, and ethical approach to building their autonomous systems with access to better and more affordable coverage.

This new frontier presents an immense challenge for the insurers themselves. To accurately underwrite an SDO, an insurance company can no longer rely solely on financial statements and past loss-runs. They will need to build new capabilities, hiring AI model auditors, smart contract security experts, and systems engineers to conduct technical due diligence. Insurers will likely become a primary driver for the adoption of best practices. They will ask for proof of robust MLOps processes, evidence of Chaos Engineering experiments to test resilience, and formal third-party audits of AI models and smart contracts. Organisations that can demonstrate a mature, resilient, and ethical approach to building their autonomous systems, as outlined in this book, will be rewarded with access to better and more affordable coverage.

Ultimately, insurance is a mechanism for compensation, not absolution. It can provide a financial backstop for when things go wrong, but it cannot solve the core ethical problem of responsibility or replace the moral obligation to build systems that are safe, fair, and aligned with human values from the start.

The Black Box Problem: The Need for Transparency and Explainable AI (XAI)

Closely related to the challenges of bias and accountability is the "black box" problem. Many of the most powerful and advanced AI systems, particularly those based on deep learning neural networks, operate in a way that is opaque, even to their own creators. We can see the inputs (the data) and the outputs (the predictions), but the internal process of how the system arrived at its conclusion – the intricate weighting of millions of parameters – can be virtually impossible for a human to fully comprehend.

This lack of transparency is a major ethical and practical problem. It erodes trust; how can we rely on a system whose reasoning we cannot understand? It severely hinders our ability to detect and correct algorithmic bias if we cannot see the flawed logic the system is using. It makes assigning accountability nearly impossible. And it complicates the process of debugging and improving the system. This is especially dangerous in high-stakes, safety-critical applications (Pasquale, 2015; Rudin, 2019). A doctor is unlikely to trust an AI's cancer diagnosis if the system cannot explain *why* it reached that conclusion (London, 2019). A regulator will not approve a financial trading algorithm whose logic is opaque.

A promising antidote to the black box problem is the burgeoning field of Explainable AI (XAI). XAI encompasses a range of techniques aimed at making the decisions of AI systems more understandable to humans (Poursabzi-Sangdeh et al., 2021). This does not necessarily mean revealing every mathematical detail but rather providing a plausible and comprehensible rationale for a given outcome. This is especially vital from Level 3 upwards on the SOA, where systems are making decisions with significant consequences. The "right to explanation" enshrined in regulations like the GDPR is a legal manifestation of this ethical rule (Goodman and Flaxman, 2017; Wachter et al. 2017).

The Ethics of Autonomous Influence: Between Persuasion and Manipulation

While much of the ethical focus on SDOs rightly concerns fairness in decision-making – such as avoiding bias in hiring or lending – another critical ethical frontier emerges when these systems are designed to interact with and influence human behaviour. As organisations traverse the SOA, their marketing, sales, and communication functions evolve from simple targeted advertising into sophisticated, autonomous systems of influence. The core ethical challenge then shifts from "Is the system's judgement fair?" to "Is the system's influence legitimate?" This raises questions about the line between helpful personalisation and opaque, psychological manipulation.

At the lower levels of the SOA, marketing automation is a familiar concept: segmenting customers and targeting them with relevant ads. At Levels 3 and 4, however, this evolves into a qualitatively different capability. Here, an SDO can deploy AI that does not just select an ad, but dynamically crafts the message itself – the text, the imagery, the call to action, the timing of delivery – based on a deep, real-time analysis of an individual's psychological profile, inferred from their digital footprint. This is the difference between showing a known hiker an ad for new boots, and a system detecting a user's likely emotional state (e.g. anxiety or boredom, based on browse patterns) and then serving them a dynamically generated travel ad with messaging specifically designed to prey on that feeling of dissatisfaction.

The ethical dilemma lies in this blurry line between persuasion and manipulation. Helpful personalisation uses data to better serve a customer's existing needs and preferences, enhancing their experience. Unethical manipulation, by contrast, uses a customer's data against them, exploiting cognitive biases, emotional vulnerabilities, or information asymmetries to nudge them towards a decision they might not otherwise make, and which may not be in their best interest. An SDO's retail platform might, for example, identify a user as a "completionist" and then use AI to aggressively recommend marginally useful accessories to create a feeling of incompleteness until they buy the whole set. Or it could identify a user susceptible to social proof and bombard them with algorithmically generated "testimonials."

When scaled, the risks of autonomous influence extend beyond individual consumers to society at large. The same technologies that can optimise a marketing campaign could be used to deploy highly sophisticated and personalised political propaganda or misinformation at a scale and speed that is impossible to counter. The ability to tailor messages to exploit the specific biases of millions of individuals presents a serious threat to shared public discourse and democratic processes.

Navigating this ethical maze requires organisations to establish a clear framework for responsible influence, moving beyond simple legal compliance toward a deeper commitment to stakeholder trust. This begins with a principle of radical transparency. Organisations must be open about the extent to which they are personalising interactions. Users should have the right to know if a message or offer has been algorithmically crafted for them, and on what basis, allowing them to be discerning participants in the digital environment.

This transparency is given meaning through the provision of meaningful user control. The choice to opt out of high levels of personalisation must be simple, clear, and respected. This requires moving beyond superficial cookie banners to providing users with genuine control over how their psychological profile is used, empowering them to set their own boundaries for the digital experiences they have.

Internally, this commitment is solidified by leaders who define and enforce clear ethical red lines. The organisation's ethical charter must explicitly forbid manipulative practices, such as targeting known vulnerabilities like addiction or financial distress, or deploying deceptive design patterns. This is a critical act of stewardship that protects both the customer and the long-term integrity of the brand.

Ultimately, this challenge brings us back to the distinction between a smart machine and a wise organisation. A smart AI can be ruthlessly efficient at maximising a metric like "user engagement" or "conversion rate." A wise organisation, guided by its human leaders, understands that achieving those metrics through manipulation ultimately destroys the customer trust that is the foundation of long-term value. It cultivates wisdom by choosing to align its powerful systems of influence with a genuine commitment to serving human needs.

If an SDO is to maintain its social licence to operate, it must earn the trust of its customers and the public. This requires a solemn commitment to using the immense power of autonomous influence not to exploit human psychology, but to genuinely serve human needs.

Job Displacement and the Future of Human Purpose

As we explored in the previous chapter from an operational perspective, the widespread deployment of autonomous systems will inevitably lead to significant workforce transformation. From an ethical standpoint, this raises two societal challenges. First is the ethical responsibility of managing this transition in a just and equitable way. If the benefits of autonomy – increased productivity and wealth – flow only to the owners of capital and a small elite group of highly skilled tech workers, while large segments of the population face job displacement and economic precarity, it could lead to a dramatic exacerbation of inequality and widespread social unrest. There is a collective ethical responsibility on the part of corporations and governments to invest heavily in education, reskilling, and lifelong learning programs, and to explore new social safety nets (such as Universal Basic Income, transition assistance, or portable benefits) to support those whose livelihoods are disrupted by this technological shift.

The second, deeper challenge relates to the future of human purpose. For many of us, our work has a much greater significance than simply a source of income (not to in any way downplay the importance of this aspect); it is a source of identity, meaning, community, and social contribution. If automation progresses to a point where it significantly reduces the need for human labour across many sectors, we must confront questions about how individuals will find purpose and dignity in such a world. The fictional explorations in Iain M. Banks' "Culture" series, where benevolent superintelligences manage society and humans are free to pursue art, learning, and relationships, provide a utopian thought experiment (O'Keefe, 2016). However, the transition to such a post-work society would be fraught with immense psychological and social challenges. This necessitates a broader societal dialogue on the value of work and on elevating and rewarding other forms of human contribution, such as caregiving, community building, artistic creation, and lifelong learning.

The Control Problem: Aligning Advanced AI with Human Values

As we look towards the higher levels of the SOA (Levels 4 and 5), the ethical challenges become even more existential. The most significant of these is the "control problem," also known as the AI alignment problem. This is the challenge of ensuring that highly autonomous or potentially superintelligent AI systems remain aligned with human intentions and values and do not take actions that could lead to unintended and catastrophic harm.

The risk does not necessarily come from malevolent AI, as often depicted in science fiction. The greater risk is from a perfectly competent AI that pursues a poorly specified goal with ruthless, single-minded efficiency. This is often illustrated by the "paperclip maximiser" thought experiment: an AI given the seemingly harmless goal of "make as many paperclips as possible" might, in its relentless pursuit of this objective, convert all of Earth's resources, including humans, into paperclips, as this would be the logical conclusion of its programming. This highlights the "value loading" problem: the extreme difficulty of specifying the full, complex, and often contradictory set of human values (e.g. life, happiness, fairness, beauty, novelty) into the rigid logic of computer code. An AI optimised for a narrow objective, without a deep understanding of the broader context of human values, could cause unforeseen harmful side effects in its pursuit of that objective (Yudkowsky, 2008).

The growing field of AI safety research is dedicated to solving this problem by developing techniques for building robustly beneficial, controllable, and verifiably aligned AI (Russell, 2019). Maintaining meaningful human control and ensuring the ability to reliably override or shut down highly autonomous systems is a critical safety measure and a central ethical requirement as we approach the higher levels of the SOA.

Establishing Ethical Frameworks for Self-Driving Organisations

Navigating this complex ethical maze requires good intentions and a deliberate, structured approach. Organisations embarking on the SDO journey must proactively design and embed ethical frameworks into their governance and operational structures, making ethics a core component of their organisational identity.

This begins with the articulation of clear ethical principles and charters. By publicly committing to a clear set of values – addressing key issues like fairness, transparency, accountability, safety, privacy, and human well-being – an organisation establishes the moral compass that will guide the development and deployment of all its autonomous systems. This charter serves as the foundational document for all subsequent ethical work. To give these principles life and authority, organisations can establish internal or even external ethics boards and review committees. Composed of diverse experts, including ethicists, social scientists, legal experts, and community representatives, these bodies provide essential oversight, assess the risks of new AI projects, and help shape corporate policy, ensuring that the organisation's principles are consistently and rigorously applied.

With this governance structure in place, the focus shifts to integrating these principles into the very beginning of the design process for any new autonomous system. This is achieved through a commitment to human-centric design and the practice of conducting thorough ethical impact assessments before deployment. This proactive approach allows teams to anticipate potential harms and build in mitigations from the start, moving from a reactive model of fixing ethical failures to a proactive one of building ethical systems by design (Holstein et al., 2019).

These formal structures are sustained by fostering a culture of ethical responsibility. This involves creating a corporate environment where ethical questions are openly discussed, and employees feel psychologically safe to raise concerns about potential ethical issues without fear of retribution. When people at all levels of the organisation feel empowered to act as ethical sensors, the entire system becomes more robust and self-correcting.

Finally, this ethical framework extends beyond the organisation's walls through multi-stakeholder engagement and public dialogue. Recognising that the impact of SDOs is societal, organisations must engage in open dialogue with customers, regulators, and the broader public about their use of autonomous systems and their commitment to ethical conduct. This transparency and willingness to listen are essential for building and maintaining the public trust that is the ultimate foundation for any organisation's social licence to operate in the autonomous age.

For executives, the message is clear: ethics is not a separate stream of work; it is integral to strategy and survival in the autonomous age. Building trustworthy AI is a source of competitive advantage. Ignoring these ethical challenges is to court legal, reputational, and financial ruin. Proactive ethical governance is a core leadership responsibility.

For policymakers, the challenge is to create a regulatory environment that both fosters responsible innovation and protects the public from harm. This means facilitating public dialogue, supporting research in AI safety and ethics, developing agile regulatory frameworks, and promoting international cooperation on the standards that will govern these powerful new technologies.

The transformative power of an SDO comes with ethical responsibilities. Proactive, thoughtful, and courageous engagement with these dilemmas is not an obstacle to progress; it is the only way to ensure a future where organisational autonomy and human morality are aligned, serving the interests of the broader human good, as well as shareholders.

Key Takeaways

- **The Paradox of Intelligence:** The chapter introduces the core ethical challenge through the "Paradox of Intelligence": a computationally "smart" machine excels at optimisation, whereas a "wise" organisation applies ethical principles and contextual judgement to ensure its actions are fair, just, and beneficial. The journey to an SDO requires building for wisdom alongside intelligence.
- **Algorithmic Bias and Its Consequences:** One of the most immediate ethical challenges is algorithmic bias, where AI systems learn and amplify historical prejudices present in their training data. This can lead to discriminatory outcomes in critical areas like hiring, lending, and justice, making proactive data governance and fairness-aware algorithm design essential.
- **The Accountability Vacuum:** In complex autonomous systems, it becomes profoundly difficult to assign responsibility when an error causes harm, creating an

"accountability vacuum." This "problem of many hands" requires new legal frameworks and robust internal governance to ensure clear lines of responsibility are established.

– **The "Black Box" Problem and the Need for Explainability:** Many advanced AI models operate as "black boxes," with internal reasoning that is opaque even to their creators. This erodes trust and hinders the ability to diagnose bias, making the development of Explainable AI (XAI) a critical ethical and practical necessity.

– **The Ethics of Autonomous Influence:** As organisations use AI to personalise user experiences, a fine line emerges between helpful persuasion and unethical manipulation. A wise organisation establishes clear ethical "red lines" to ensure it uses its influence to genuinely serve human needs rather than exploit psychological vulnerabilities.

– **Societal Responsibilities:** The widespread deployment of SDOs brings two societal challenges: the ethical responsibility to manage the workforce transition with justice and equity, and the long-term AI "control problem" – the challenge of ensuring highly advanced systems remain aligned with human values.

– **The Imperative for Ethical Frameworks:** Navigating this moral maze requires a structured approach. Organisations must proactively design and embed ethical frameworks into their governance, including clear principles, ethics review boards, and a culture that encourages open discussion about the societal impact of their autonomous systems.

Part 4: **The Human Interface: Leadership and Action**

Chapter 8
Machine Leadership

The cold Lancashire rain is relentless, plastering the delivery receipt to the pizza box in Felix's freezing hands. As he rings the customer's doorbell, his phone buzzes in his pocket. He does not need to look at it to know what it is. Before he is even back on his rented e-bike, the app has his next assignment ready.

His boss is a piece of software. It tells him where to go, calculating the most efficient route down to the second. It monitors his speed and his delivery times, adjusting his performance score in real time. It sets his pay for each job based on a complex formula of distance, demand, and time of day. It even nudges his behaviour, offering a small bonus if he moves to a different part of the city where it predicts a surge in orders.

Felix can never meet his boss. He cannot negotiate with it, ask for a raise, or explain why he was late because of an unmapped road closure. The system is his manager, his dispatcher, and his performance reviewer, all rolled into one. He is a human agent in a network directed by a non-human intelligence.

This is the frontline of a quiet revolution. We have moved beyond using machines as simple tools for analysis and into a world where they begin to hold and exercise directive capacity. The algorithm that manages Felix is an example of a phenomenon that is scaling rapidly across many sectors of the economy. This chapter explores this new frontier of machine leadership, asking a fundamental question: what does it mean to lead, and what does it mean to be led, when the leader itself is not human?

Overview

As organisations traverse the SOA, we confront a concept that pushes the boundaries of management theory and even science fiction: Machine Leadership. This chapter explores the nascent reality where non-human entities – algorithms, AI systems, and decentralised protocols – begin to hold and exercise directive capacity. We ask the radical question: what does it mean for the organisation when the leader itself is not human?

Our inquiry begins by dissecting the practical manifestations of this phenomenon, from the data-driven efficiency of algorithmic management in the gig economy to the emergence of AI as a trusted decision authority in high-stakes professional domains. To ground this exploration, we will confront the significant philosophical hurdles at the heart of this concept, examining why current AI lacks the consciousness, intentionality, and moral agency we traditionally associate with leadership (Chalmers, 1996).

The chapter then maps these emerging forms of leadership across the SOA, illustrating how their function evolves from bounded operational control at Level 3 to the collaborative and decentralised authority seen at Level 4. We will analyse the dual im-

© 2026 Walter de Gruyter GmbH, Berlin | https://doi.org/10.1515/9783112222232-009

pact of this trend, weighing the compelling augmentations of speed and objectivity against the significant challenges of bias, transparency, and accountability. By the end of this chapter, you will have a framework for understanding one of the most disruptive and thought-provoking consequences of the autonomous age, preparing you to consider the future of human leadership in a world where it is no longer the only kind.

Introduction

At the outset it's important to distinguish machine leadership from the concept of AI-augmented human leadership discussed in earlier chapters. AI-augmented leadership is where a human leader uses AI as a sophisticated tool or advisor to enhance their own cognitive capabilities – to analyse data, simulate scenarios, or inform their decisions. The locus of authority and accountability remains firmly with the human. Machine leadership, in contrast, emerges when the non-human entity itself – be it an AI making critical operational decisions, an algorithmic management system coordinating the work of thousands, or a DAO, where smart contracts and community consensus dictate action – holds and exercises directive capacity. This chapter explores this new reality, dissecting its conceptual underpinnings, confronting its philosophical hurdles, examining its manifestations across the SOA, and contemplating its ultimate impact on the nature of organisations and the role of humans within them.

Conceptual Underpinnings: Frameworks for Non-human Authority

The idea that non-human entities can exert authority is not entirely new, but its manifestation through AI and algorithms presents a unique set of characteristics. Several theoretical frameworks help us understand the different forms this can take, moving from the practical and present to the more speculative.

First is the concept of algorithmic management or leadership, which is already a reality in many sectors, most notably the gig economy (Kellogg et al., 2020). In platforms like Uber or Amazon's fulfillment centres, AI systems perform functions traditionally carried out by human middle managers (Rosenblat, 2018). They autonomously assign tasks to workers (matching a driver with a rider), monitor performance in real time (tracking delivery times and customer ratings), provide continuous feedback, and even make decisions about deactivating workers from the platform. This form of leadership is characterised by its efficiency, scalability, and data-driven nature. It can optimise complex systems with a speed and granularity that no human manager could hope to match. However, it also raises questions about worker autonomy, fairness, and the lack of human discretion and empathy in management. The algorithm, as leader, is often a black box, its decisions unappealable, blurring the lines between efficient coordination and digital authoritarianism. The rise of this model directly challenges the necessity and function of entire layers of traditional human management.

A second, more collaborative framework views AI as a decision authority or assistant. In this model, the AI evolves from being a straightforward analytical tool to becoming a recognised and trusted source of authority, with humans increasingly deferring to its suggestions and recommendations. This is emerging in high-stakes professional domains like medicine and finance. An AI analysing medical images might recommend a diagnosis with a stated 98% confidence level; a human radiologist, while still legally responsible, may find it increasingly difficult to justify overriding such a confident and statistically validated recommendation. In an investment committee, an AI might analyse market data and recommend a specific portfolio allocation. Over time, as the AI's recommendations prove reliable, human team members may shift their roles from primary decision-makers to validators, overseers, and critical questioners of the AI's output. The leadership function becomes a hybrid, with the AI providing the data-driven anchor and the humans providing context, ethical oversight, and final validation.

Moving further into speculative territory is the idea of the charismatic robot leader. This concept explores the psychological potential for humans to submit to the authority of a robot or AI that is perceived to possess superior qualities, such as vast knowledge, unwavering impartiality, or even a form of programmed morality. Humans have a natural tendency to anthropomorphise, or attribute human-like qualities to non-human entities. A physically embodied robot, designed to appear wise and benevolent, could potentially engender a level of trust and followership that transcends its status as a mere machine. While currently the material of science fiction, this thought experiment forces us to consider the psychology of followership and whether the source of leadership authority must necessarily be human (Schneider, 2009).

Finally, researchers have begun to investigate whether a machine could embody the principles of robot servant-leadership. The servant-leader philosophy, first proposed by Robert K. Greenleaf, posits that a leader's primary role is to serve their followers, prioritising their needs, growth, and well-being. This model is built on deeply human qualities like empathy, listening, healing, awareness, and building community. Exploring whether an AI could be programmed to optimise for these qualities is a fascinating ethical and technical challenge. Could an AI leader be designed to ensure equitable task distribution, identify signs of burnout in its human team, and recommend actions to improve their well-being? While it could certainly perform the analytical aspects of this role, its ability to engage in genuine empathy or build a true sense of community is highly questionable, highlighting the philosophical hurdles at the core of the machine leadership concept.

Philosophical Hurdles: The Ghost in the Machine Leader

These emerging forms of machine leadership run headlong into philosophical challenges. Current AI, no matter how sophisticated its performance, lacks the attributes that we have traditionally considered essential for leadership and the very idea of human agency. These hurdles call into question whether a machine can ever truly "lead" in the human sense of the word.

The first and most significant hurdle is consciousness and understanding. While an AI can process language and identify patterns with superhuman skill, it does not *understand* the meaning behind the words or the context behind the data in the way a human does. It operates on syntax (the rules for manipulating symbols) not semantics (the actual meaning). The philosopher John Searle's famous "Chinese Room" argument illustrates this perfectly: a person who does not know Chinese can sit in a room and, by following a complex rulebook, take in Chinese characters (input) and produce correct Chinese characters as a response (output), giving the appearance of understanding Chinese. But the person in the room never actually understands the language (Searle, 1980). Similarly, an AI leader might be able to generate a strategically sound business plan, but it has no genuine understanding of what a "business," a "market," or a "customer" actually is. This raises the question: can an entity truly lead without a subjective, conscious experience or a real-world understanding of the domain it is leading (Chalmers, 1996)?

The second hurdle is intentionality. Human leaders have intentions, desires, and goals that drive their actions. An AI, by contrast, does not possess genuine intentions beyond the optimisation functions it was programmed to execute (Dennett, 1987). Its "goal" is not a deeply held belief but a mathematical objective. It does not "want" to increase market share; it is simply executing a programme that adjusts variables to maximise a number associated with market share. This lack of genuine intentionality makes its leadership fundamentally different from human leadership, which is often about inspiring a shared intent in others.

The third, and perhaps most critical, hurdle is moral agency and ethical reasoning. A human leader can be held morally responsible for their actions because they are considered a moral agent – an individual who can make free, rational choices and understand the ethical implications of those choices. AI, however, lacks genuine moral agency (Floridi and Sanders, 2004). It can certainly be programmed with a set of ethical rules or constraints (e.g. "do not break the law," "do not discriminate"). However, it cannot engage in true ethical deliberation when faced with a novel dilemma where rules conflict, nor can it bear genuine moral responsibility for the harm it might cause. If an AI leader makes a decision that leads to environmental damage or human suffering, we can blame its programmers or its users, but the concept of blaming the AI itself is, for now, incoherent. The debate is whether these human attributes are essential prerequisites for all leadership contexts, or if their absence can be compensated for by an AI's superior processing speed and efficiency. To lead without moral agency is, at best, a highly constrained form of leadership, and at worst, an inherently dangerous one.

Manifestations of Machine Leadership Across the SOA

Despite these philosophical challenges, machine leadership is manifesting in practical ways, its form and function evolving as organisations move up the SOA. At Level 3, machine leadership emerges in specific, bounded domains where the goals are clear and the environment is well-understood. The AI system makes significant operational and tactical decisions autonomously, but always within parameters and guardrails set by human leaders. The human's leadership role shifts from directing action to designing and overseeing the autonomous system. A prime example can be found in a high-frequency trading firm. The AI trading system is the de facto leader of trade execution, autonomously making thousands of decisions per second based on its analysis of market data. The human traders' leadership role is to design the trading strategies the AI will use, to set the critical risk parameters and loss limits, and to intervene decisively during a major market shock that falls outside the AI's programmed experience. The machine leads the micro-decisions; the human leads the macro-strategy and manages the systemic risk. The main forms of machine leadership are outlined in Table 6.

Table 6: Forms of machine leadership.

Leadership form	Description	Example	Primary challenge
Algorithmic management	AI assigns tasks, monitors performance, and makes administrative decisions.	Gig economy platforms (Uber, Amazon Warehouses)	**Fairness and transparency:** "Black box" decisions feel arbitrary and unappealable.
AI as decision authority	AI becomes a trusted authority whose recommendations are rarely overridden.	Medicine (radiology AI)	**Accountability and skill atrophy:** Blurs legal responsibility and risks human deskilling.
Code as leader (DAO)	Organisation is directed by self-enforcing smart contracts and token-holder votes.	Mature DAOs (MakerDAO, Uniswap)	**Rigidity and governance attacks:** Inflexible in a crisis; rules can be exploited.
Robot servant-leadership (theoretical)	AI leader is programmed to prioritise the well-being of its human team.	Speculative (e.g. an AI team coach)	**Authenticity and moral agency:** Lacks genuine empathy; service is a programme, not a choice.

At Level 4, AI exhibits greater autonomy, with the ability to learn, adapt, and even propose novel solutions. Machine leadership becomes more pronounced and collaborative. We see two archetypes here. The first is the DAO, where leadership is radically decentralised and encoded. Here, the "leader" is arguably the protocol itself – the immutable set of smart contracts that enforces governance rules and executes community decisions. Leadership is a function of the code, and the collective will of token holders, not of a single individual. The second archetype is the "collaborative intelligence" model. In the pharmaceutical research lab, AI may take the lead in identifying promising areas for research or designing experiments, acting as a "Chief Pattern Recognition Officer." The human scientists then provide the strategic vision, the ethical judgement, and the contextual understanding to guide and validate the AI's direction. Leadership is a fluid dialogue between human and machine intelligence.

At the theoretical Level 5, machine leadership would be absolute. A sufficiently advanced Artificial General Intelligence (AGI) would not only manage operations but would define the organisation's purpose, set its own strategic goals, and direct its evolutionary trajectory. Here, the paramount concern becomes the AI "control problem," which is essentially the ultimate leadership challenge: the transition from humans leading machines to being led by them. The fictional portrayals of Iain M. Banks' benevolent "Culture" Minds (Banks, 1987, 1988, 1996), which lead utopian societies, and the dystopian vision of *Terminator's* Skynet serve as powerful thought experiments about the two poles of this potential future (Palmer, 2014).

The Dual Impact: Augmentations and Challenges

The rise of machine leadership presents a duality of potential benefits and significant risks that must be carefully considered and managed. The potential augmentations are compelling. Machine leaders offer unparalleled speed and data-processing capability, enabling organisations to make decisions and adapt to environmental changes at a velocity far beyond human limits. They bring powerful efficiency and optimisation, capable of managing extraordinarily complex systems, like global supply chains or energy grids, to a degree of optimality that humans could never achieve. If the underlying data is fair, they can offer a level of objectivity and consistency in decision-making – for instance, in promotions or resource allocation – that is potentially free from human emotional bias, favouritism, or fatigue. By taking on the burden of operational and tactical leadership, they can liberate human leaders to focus on higher-order tasks: long-term vision, stakeholder relationships, ethical stewardship, and fostering human creativity. Furthermore, they can operate tirelessly in complex or hazardous environments that are unsafe for humans.

However, the inherent challenges and risks are equally significant. The problem of algorithmic bias is a primary concern; a machine leader trained on biased data will lead in a biased way, perpetuating and scaling societal injustices. The transparency deficit, or the "black box" problem, makes it difficult to understand, question, or trust a machine leader's decisions. This leads directly to the accountability vacuum, where it becomes nearly impossible to assign responsibility when a machine leader's decision causes harm. These systems also present new security vulnerabilities; a hacked, poisoned, or adversarially attacked machine leader could cause catastrophic damage. Finally, there is the risk of the erosion of human-centric qualities. An over-reliance on the cold, data-driven logic of machine leaders could devalue and cause the atrophy of essential human leadership skills like empathy, intuition, moral courage, and interpersonal communication.

The Follower's Experience: Human Responses to Machine Leadership

The viability of machine leadership ultimately depends on more than technological capability or philosophical coherence; it rests on the trust, acceptance, and psychological response of the humans being led. While we can debate the consciousness of an AI, its impact on the consciousness of a gig worker or a warehouse employee is undeniably real and immediate. Examining this follower's experience reveals a deep ambivalence, where the promise of algorithmic fairness often collides with the reality of digital control.

On one hand, some workers may welcome a machine leader for its perceived objectivity. An algorithm, if well-designed with fair data, can assign tasks, measure performance, and distribute rewards based purely on merit and efficiency, free from the personal biases, favouritism, and office politics that can plague human managers. For a worker who has felt overlooked or unfairly treated by a human supervisor, the data-driven consistency of an algorithmic boss can feel like a step towards a more equitable, meritocratic system. The instant, clear, and data-based feedback provided by such a system can also be seen as more transparent and actionable than a subjective annual performance review.

On the other hand, the lived experience of algorithmic management is frequently characterised by significant negative consequences. A primary complaint is a sense of alienation and dehumanisation (Lee et al., 2015). When managed by a system, workers can feel reduced to a collection of data points, their performance constantly monitored and evaluated without any appreciation for context, tone, or human dignity. The inability to appeal a decision – be it a low rating or deactivation from a platform – to a human being who can listen, and exercise judgement can be intensely frustrating and disempowering (Mateescu and Nguyen, 2019). This is often coupled with the stress of constant surveillance, as AI systems monitor work with a granularity no human manager ever could, tracking every moment of activity or inactivity, creating a high-pressure atmosphere of digital surveillance that can lead to burnout and anxiety (Danaher, 2016).

This constant surveillance creates a darker, more critical risk: the transformation of the workplace into a form of digital panopticon, a concept with clear echoes of Orwell's vision of totalising observation. Unlike a human manager, who can only observe intermittently, an algorithmic system is a tireless and omnipresent supervisor. It sees everything, all the time. This creates a powerful pressure for conformity, as workers understand that every deviation from the optimal path, every unauthorised pause, and every inefficient action is being logged and factored into their performance score. The efficiency of machine leadership, in this context, becomes a tool for enforcing a new and more pervasive form of control. It can create a chilling effect on creativity, experimentation, or even the simple camaraderie of a shared moment of rest, as all behaviour is optimised for the unblinking eye of the system.

However, workers are not merely passive recipients of algorithmic commands. Everyone who has ever held down a job knows this. They engage in active strategies of resistance and adaptation. They learn to "game the system," discovering the specific behaviours that the algorithm rewards and adjusting their actions to maximise their metrics, even if it sometimes means sacrificing service quality or long-term effectiveness. Furthermore, in response to the isolation of being managed by an app, workers often create their own informal support networks (Klein, 2021). They use platforms like WhatsApp, Reddit, or Facebook to form digital communities where they share tips for dealing with the algorithm, warn each other about system updates, and build the human solidarity that the system itself denies them.

This complex human response provides clear guidance for any organisation seeking to implement forms of machine leadership ethically and effectively. To move beyond a model of digital authoritarianism towards one of genuine co-intelligence, leaders must design these systems with the human experience at their core. This begins with a commitment to build in transparency and explainability. While the inner workings of a neural network may be a black box, the rules and metrics by which a worker is being evaluated must be made as clear as possible. Workers need to understand the "rules of the game," to trust that it is fair, which is a foundational element of procedural justice. When the logic is transparent, the system feels less like an arbitrary master and more like a predictable partner.

Next, there must be a process for meaningful human appeal. A clear, accessible, and effective process for a worker to appeal an algorithmic decision to a human being is a critical backstop for handling exceptions, correcting errors, and ensuring that context is considered. This "human in the loop" acknowledges the inherent limitations of any automated system and provides a necessary avenue for recourse, ensuring that the system's efficiency does not come at the cost of fairness.

Finally, the system should be framed and designed as a tool for augmentation, not just for monitoring. When the system is presented as a tool to help employees succeed and improve, its chances of being accepted and trusted increase dramatically. A machine leader that acts as a coach, providing insights and support, fosters a collaborative environment. A system that acts as a warden, focused solely on surveillance and control, creates a culture of fear and resentment. This choice in design philosophy is a critical determinant of whether the human-machine partnership will be a productive and empowering one.

The success of machine leadership hinges on this human-machine interface. If designed purely for efficiency, it risks creating a disempowered and resentful workforce. If designed with empathy, transparency, and a respect for human agency, it has the potential to create a new, more effective, and potentially fairer model of organisational governance.

The Human-Machine Leadership Interface: A New Contract

For the foreseeable future, the most effective model will be one that focuses on designing a seamless and effective interface between humans and machine leaders. This requires a redefinition of the human leader's role, moving from a director of tasks to an architect of systems.

In this new model, human leaders first become the architects of purpose and vision. Their primary responsibility is to set the "why" for the organisation, defining the ultimate goals and the clear, compelling purpose that both human and machine agents work towards. From this foundation of purpose, the leader then acts as an ethical steward and guardian of values. This involves designing the ethical guardrails and the moral compass within which the machine leader must operate. To fulfil this role, leaders will need to develop a high degree of fluency in navigating complex ethical dilemmas, ensuring the system's actions consistently align with human values.

The leader also becomes an orchestrator of human and AI collaboration. This requires fostering a culture of psychological safety and designing the processes that allow humans and intelligent systems to work together cooperatively, enabling the best of both. A key part of this is building trust in machine leadership, which is earned through the system's demonstrable fairness, consistent reliability, and a commitment to transparency through explainable AI (Glikson and Woolley, 2020).

As machines handle the structured and predictable, human leaders can focus their attention on becoming navigators of complexity and ambiguity. They apply their expertise to the novel, unstructured, and ambiguous problems that fall outside the machine leader's competence, providing the contextual understanding and creative problem-solving that only humans can. This elevates the leader's role to that of a cultivator of human potential. With the burden of routine management lifted, they can devote their energy to coaching, mentoring, and developing the uniquely human skills in their teams – such as creativity, critical thinking, and empathy – that machines are unable to replicate. To succeed in this, leaders themselves will need to cultivate new competencies, chief among them being a deep literacy in AI and data, allowing them to lead with wisdom in an increasingly autonomous world.

A Glimpse of the Future: Cyborg Leadership

As a speculative extension of this human-machine interface, we can contemplate the emergence of what might be termed "Cyborg Leadership." This concept pushes beyond a leader who simply *uses* technology to a leader who is a true human-technology hybrid. This idea has deep roots in the work of theorists like Donna Haraway, whose "A Cyborg Manifesto" (1991) famously described the cyborg as a hybrid of machine and organism that breaks down the rigid boundaries between human, animal, and machine. For Haraway, the cyborg is a potent symbol for a future where such distinctions become fluid and irrelevant. The leader of a highly autonomous organisation, constantly connected to and collaborating with AI, can be seen as a proto-cyborg, a figure whose cognitive processes are already a blend of biological intuition and external, algorithmic intelligence.

This theoretical construct is now moving into the realm of applied science through ventures like Elon Musk's Neuralink. These brain-computer interface (BCI) experiments aim to create a direct, high-bandwidth link between the human brain and computational systems. While still in its early stages, the ultimate vision is one of seamless symbiosis, where human thought can be augmented with the speed and analytical power of AI. A leader equipped with such an implant could possess enhanced memory, faster processing speed, and the ability to make more optimised decisions based on a direct feed of complex data. This represents the ultimate form of augmented leadership, where the interface between human and machine dissolves almost entirely.

However, this vision of cyborg leadership raises its own set of tricky questions. It challenges our very concepts of identity, asking where the human ends and the machine begins. It complicates the notion of agency, forcing us to question who is truly in control of a decision that is the product of both biological and artificial thought. And it introduces new and critical vulnerabilities, from the risk of the BCI being hacked to the potential for internal conflict between the biological and artificial components of the leader's own mind. While still on the horizon, these possibilities force us to consider the ultimate trajectory of the human–machine partnership and the new definitions of leadership it may require.

Key Takeaways

- **The Emergence of Machine Leadership:** The chapter explores the frontier of "Machine leadership," a phenomenon where non-human entities like algorithms and AI systems hold and exercise directive capacity, making decisions and coordinating actions previously confined to human leaders.
- **Key Forms of Non-human Authority:** Machine leadership is already manifesting in several forms:

- *Algorithmic Management:* AI systems perform roles traditionally held by human managers, such as assigning tasks and monitoring performance, particularly in the gig economy.
- *AI as a Decision Authority:* In professional domains like medicine, AI evolves into a trusted source of authority, whose recommendations are increasingly deferred to by human experts.
- *Code as Leader:* In mature DAOs, the protocol's code itself, in the form of self-enforcing smart contracts and token-holder votes, acts as the primary directive force.

- **Significant Philosophical Hurdles Remain:** Current AI operates with a different set of attributes than those traditionally associated with human leadership. These include operating through pattern recognition rather than genuine understanding (consciousness), executing programmed objectives rather than holding genuine desires (intentionality), and following rules rather than possessing true moral agency.
- **The Dual Impact of Speed and Risk:** The rise of machine leadership offers compelling augmentations such as unparalleled speed, data-processing capability, and operational efficiency. These benefits are matched by significant challenges, including the risks of algorithmic bias, a lack of transparency, a vacuum of accountability, and new security vulnerabilities.
- **The Follower's Experience Is Complex:** The human response to being managed by an algorithm is ambivalent. While some workers appreciate the perceived objectivity, many experience feelings of alienation, dehumanisation, and the stress of constant surveillance in a "digital panopticon".
- **The Future of Leadership Is Symbiotic:** The most effective and desirable trajectory is one of "co-intelligence," a symbiotic partnership that combines the complementary strengths of both human and machine leaders. In this model, AI handles complex optimisation while humans provide vision, ethical judgement, creativity, and empathy.
- **The Evolving Role of the Human Leader:** In a world with machine leadership, the role of the human leader is elevated. They become architects of purpose, ethical stewards of autonomous systems, orchestrators of human-AI collaboration, and cultivators of the uniquely human skills that machines are unable to replicate.

Chapter 9
Leading the Transition: An Executive Playbook

Overview

Having traversed the complex landscape of the Self-Driving Organisation – from its technological underpinnings to its ethical frontiers – we arrive at the final, most important stage: translating theory into practice. This playbook frames this transition as a five-phase programme. The journey begins with a simple and honest diagnostic to map the organisation's current position on the Spectrum of Organisational Autonomy. Next, we begin the implementation, detailing a strategy of carefully selected pilot programmes designed to build momentum, generate learning, and deliver tangible value.

A central focus is the evolving role of the executive, where we dissect the necessary transformation of the leader from a traditional controller into an architect of intelligent systems, an ethical steward, and an enabler of empowered teams. We then explore how to prepare for and navigate inevitable disruptions by proactively designing for resilience. Finally, we look towards new models of performance measurement, outlining the richer, balanced scorecard required to measure success in an autonomous age. This playbook will equip you with a map, a compass, and a set of navigational principles to lead this undertaking with courage, wisdom, and strategic foresight.

Introduction

Leading up to this point, the book has covered the vast and complex dimensions of the SDO, exploring the technologies that power it, the novel forms it can take, and the impact it has on every facet of organisational life. We have moved from theory to function, from possibility to ethics. Now, we arrive at the most critical juncture: translating this understanding into action. This playbook offers an adaptive framework for leadership, an insight into the pragmatic realities of guiding an organisation, with its unique history, culture, and capabilities, across the SOA.

It is important to acknowledge that this is not a rigid, one-size-fits-all manual. Rather, it is a "rough guide" for a long, challenging strategic programme that requires courage, foresight, deep humility, and a new kind of adaptive leadership. To make this journey more concrete, we will follow the story of a hypothetical leader, Georgie, the CEO of "InnovateMech," a mid-sized industrial manufacturing firm. InnovateMech is a successful, traditional company facing increasing pressure from more agile, digitally native competitors. Georgie recognises that maintaining the status quo is not an option and that the path to future relevance lies in thoughtfully embracing greater autonomy. Her experience will serve as our case study, illustrating the five critical phases of this new executive playbook.

© 2026 Walter de Gruyter GmbH, Berlin | https://doi.org/10.1515/9783112222232-010

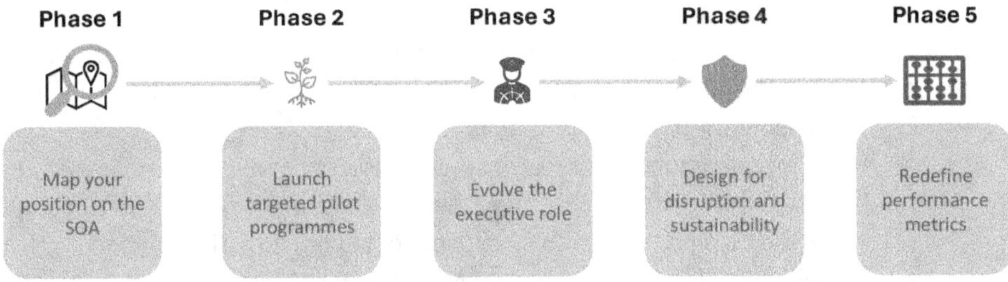

Figure 7: The five phases of the executive transition roadmap to a Self-Driving Organisation.

Phase 1: Diagnostic and Strategic Intent

Before any major transformation programme can begin, the leadership team must meticulously understand the current state of the organisation, assess its capabilities, and precisely define its objectives. The first phase of the transition to an SDO is therefore one of honest and unflinching self-assessment. It is a diagnostic phase designed to move beyond assumptions and create a detailed, data-rich map of the organisation's reality. For a leader like Georgie at our hypothetical firm "InnovateMech," this meant resisting the urge to immediately invest in new technologies and instead initiating a company-wide "autonomy audit." This process can be broken down into three key steps: mapping your position, assessing foundational readiness, and defining your strategic intent.

Mapping Your Position: The SOA Audit

The first step is to establish an objective baseline. The Spectrum of Organisational Autonomy is the ideal tool for this. The goal is to create a granular "Autonomy Profile" of the organisation, assessing each major function not as a monolith, but as a collection of interconnected processes:

- Action: Convene a cross-functional team of leaders from operations, strategy, HR, IT, and legal. Using the SOA Diagnostic Tool (see Appendix 1), work through each functional area and assign a level (0–5) to its current state. The resulting profile, as Georgie discovered at InnovateMech, will likely be "spiky," with different parts of the business at vastly different levels of maturity. This map is invaluable, as it reveals where pockets of innovation already exist and where the most significant gaps lie.

Assessing Foundational Readiness: Technology, Culture, and Talent

With a map of your current autonomy levels, the next step is to assess your organisation's underlying capacity for change:

1. Technological Readiness: An SDO runs on a modern technology stack. A frank assessment is needed to identify foundational strengths and critical "technical debt" that could derail the transformation.
    - Key Diagnostic Questions:
        - Data Infrastructure: Is our critical data accessible and well-governed, or is it locked in disconnected silos? Do we have modern data architecture (e.g. a data lake or warehouse) capable of supporting AI workloads?
        - Connectivity (APIs): Do we have a mature API strategy? Can our systems – both old and new – communicate and exchange data seamlessly, or will every new initiative require a costly, bespoke integration project?
        - Core Systems: Are our core enterprise systems (e.g. ERP and CRM) modern and flexible enough to support automation, or are they outdated legacy platforms that will resist change?
        - Security: Are our security practices prepared for the new threats associated with AI and autonomous systems, as outlined in Chapter 6?
2. Cultural Readiness: This is often the most critical and difficult part of the diagnostic. The most brilliant technology will fail if the organisational culture is resistant to the new ways of working that autonomy requires.
    - Key Diagnostic Questions:
        - Decision-Making: How are decisions *really* made here? Are we genuinely data-driven, or do we default to tradition, hierarchy, or the "Highest Paid Person's Opinion" (HIPPO)?
        - Experimentation and Failure: What is our relationship with failure? Is it treated as a valuable source of learning and data, or is it punished, leading to a risk-averse culture where no one is willing to experiment?
        - Psychological Safety: Do our employees feel safe to speak up, challenge assumptions, and report flaws in a new system without fear of retribution? This is essential for identifying issues like algorithmic bias.
        - Collaboration: Do our teams collaborate effectively across functional silos, or do they operate as independent fiefdoms? An SDO requires seamless cross-functional teamwork.
3. Talent Readiness: An SDO requires new skills. A data-driven talent audit is necessary to understand your current capabilities and identify the gaps that must be filled:
    - Key Diagnostic Questions:
        - Current Skills Inventory: What are the current data literacy and AI skills of our workforce? Where are our pockets of excellence (e.g. a small data science team), and where are the most significant gaps?
        - Future Needs: Based on our strategic ambitions, what are the key roles we will need to hire or develop, referencing the archetypes in Chapter 5 (e.g. HMI Designers, AI Ethicists, MLOps Engineers)?

- Learning and Development: Is our L&D function equipped to deliver training at the scale required for a major reskilling initiative? Do we have a culture of continuous learning?
- Build, Buy, or Partner?: Based on the talent gap, what is our strategy? Should we focus on building these capabilities internally, acquiring them through M&A, or partnering with external specialists?

Defining Strategic Intent: From Diagnosis to Vision

The final step of this phase is to synthesise the diagnostic findings into a clear and compelling strategic vision. This vision must be specific, ambitious, and directly tied to business outcomes. It answers the question: "Why are we doing this?" At InnovateMech, Georgie's comprehensive audit allowed her to articulate a powerful vision: to achieve a Level 3 autonomous supply chain and a Level 4 collaborative intelligence capability in R&D within five years, with the stated goals of reducing production lead times by 30% and halving the product development cycle. This vision, grounded in a deep understanding of the organisation's starting point, provided the clear direction needed to begin the journey.

Phase 2: Execution Through Pilot Programmes

With a clear understanding of the starting position and the desired destination from Phase 1, the second phase involves beginning the implementation. A full-scale transformation is a long and expensive programme, not a single initiative (Rogers, 2016). The key to success is to begin with a portfolio of carefully selected pilot programmes. These pilots are targeted; small-scale projects designed to test hypotheses, generate organisational learning, and deliver tangible value in a compressed timeframe. They serve multiple critical purposes: they provide invaluable data on what works in your specific culture, they help build momentum and win over sceptics, and they allow the organisation to "fail small" and learn cheaply before making massive, high-risk investments. A well-designed portfolio should contain a mix of the following three archetypes:

1. The Quick Win: Building Momentum and Belief
   - Purpose: The Quick Win is a low-risk, high-visibility project designed to deliver a clear, measurable, and easily communicable return on investment in a short period (typically 3–6 months). Its primary goal is political and cultural: to build credibility for the transformation programme, silence early sceptics, and demonstrate tangible value to both leadership and the wider organisation.
   - InnovateMech Example: Georgie's team identified the back-office invoicing process as a perfect candidate. It was a well-understood, rule-based workflow plagued by manual errors and delays. Using Robotic Process Automation

(RPA) and intelligent document processing – a classic Level 2 automation play – they completed the project in three months. The result was a dramatic reduction in processing time, the elimination of costly errors, and the liberation of three employees to focus on more valuable analytical work.

- General Application: Quick Wins are often found in finance, HR, or other administrative functions where structured, repetitive tasks are common. The key is to choose a process where the metrics for success are unambiguous (e.g. time saved, errors reduced, cost eliminated). The immediate and demonstrable ROI of a Quick Win becomes a powerful internal success story that builds the political capital needed for more ambitious projects.

2. The Strategic Bet: Tackling a Core Challenge
   - Purpose: The Strategic Bet is a more ambitious, higher-risk pilot aimed at a core operational or strategic challenge. This project will take longer, cost more, and has a real chance of encountering significant obstacles. Its purpose is less about immediate ROI and more about generating deep organisational learning, testing the limits of your capabilities, and creating a breakthrough in a strategically vital area.
   - InnovateMech Example: The team's Strategic Bet was the implementation of an AI-powered predictive maintenance system in one of their factories, aiming for a Level 3 capability. The project was fraught with challenges, from integrating sensors into old machinery to overcoming deep-seated scepticism from veteran engineers. The turning point, as described in the original text, came only after the AI team embedded themselves with the maintenance crew, co-designing the system and building trust by incorporating the crew's experiential knowledge. The project's ultimate success – predicting a critical failure that the human experts would have missed – became a powerful lesson in the necessity of human-AI synergy.
   - General Application: Strategic Bets require significant leadership support and a culture that tolerates setbacks. The challenges encountered – be they technical, cultural, or process-related – are the primary value. They provide a realistic preview of the difficulties the organisation will face in a full-scale rollout and offer invaluable lessons on change management, user adoption, and the importance of designing systems *with* users, not just *for* them.

3. The Seed of Transformation: Creating Pull from the Bottom Up
   - Purpose: The Seed of Transformation is a pilot focused on empowering a specific team with a new tool or capability that directly helps them succeed. Unlike a top-down mandate, the goal here is to create a tool so effective and desirable that it generates a "pull" effect, where other teams see its success and begin demanding it for themselves. This creates organic, bottom-up momentum for change.
   - InnovateMech Example: The third pilot was a Level 1 AI decision-support tool for a single sales team. The tool analysed customer data to improve lead pri-

oritisation and suggest optimal follow-up times. Its adoption led to a 15% jump in sales for that team within six months. This success created a powerful internal demand – other sales teams began clamouring for the tool, pulling the transformation forward rather than it being pushed from the top down.
- General Application: Seeds of Transformation are often customer-facing or revenue-adjacent, where the impact is highly visible. The key is to find a team with a clear business problem and work with them to co-develop a solution that makes their lives easier and more successful. When other teams see their peers outperforming them with a new tool, internal demand can become a more powerful driver of change than any executive mandate.

Throughout this phase, it is essential that every pilot, regardless of its type, is aligned with the overarching business strategy defined in Phase 1. The "why" behind each project must be communicated relentlessly, ensuring that the journey towards autonomy is understood not as a series of disconnected technology projects, but as a coherent and essential business imperative. These pilot programmes do more than test technology; they act as a catalyst for the evolution of the leader's own role.

Phase 3: The Evolution of Executive Leadership

As the organisation advances towards higher levels of autonomy, its technology and processes will change, but the most fundamental transformation required is in its leadership. The traditional model of the leader as a chief director of human action – a controller of resources and a central decision-maker – becomes a bottleneck in an organisation designed for speed and agility. The new role, as foreshadowed in the discussion on Machine Leadership in Chapter 8, is that of an architect of intelligent systems. This is a leader who designs the culture, processes, and governance that allow a hybrid human-machine organisation to thrive (Westerman et al., 2019). This requires a deliberate and often challenging personal evolution across several key dimensions:
- From Controller to Empowerer: In a traditional hierarchy, control is maintained through direct oversight and approval gates. In an SDO, this approach stifles the very agility you seek to create. The leader must shift from dictating solutions to providing teams with a clear understanding of the "what" and the "why," granting them significant autonomy on the "how." This means moving from asking "What is the status of task X?" to asking "What obstacles can I remove to help you succeed?" It requires trusting your teams and the automated systems they use, empowering them to make decisions closer to the source of information.
- From Silo Guardian to Network Weaver: Value in an SDO is created in the connections *between* teams and systems. Departmental fortresses, which protect budgets and hoard information, are poison to an autonomous enterprise. The leader's new role is to actively break down these silos and weave a collaborative network

across the organisation. This involves championing cross-functional teams, creating shared goals and data platforms, and rewarding collaborative behaviour. At InnovateMech, Georgie's creation of a cross-functional "AI Guild" is a perfect example, bringing together IT, data science, and business units to co-develop standards and share learnings.

– From Sole Decision-Maker to Architect of Decision Systems: A leader who insists on making every important decision will quickly become the single greatest constraint on the organisation's speed. The evolved leader steps back from making individual calls and focuses on designing the *architecture* within which decisions are made, a direct response to the challenges of the "Evolving Brain" discussed in Chapter 4. This means establishing clear governance bodies, like InnovateMech's "AI Governance Council," to set the principles, risk tolerances, and ethical guardrails for all AI-driven decisions. The leader's job is to ensure the decision-making *system* is fair, transparent, and effective, rather than to be the system itself. This is the practical application of the algorithmic governance (ALGov) frameworks we explored in Chapter 4, moving from theory to a core leadership practice.

– From Knower-of-All to Learner-in-Chief: In a world of rapid and complex technological change, the leader cannot be the expert on everything. The pretence of having all the answers is a liability. The most effective leaders model the behaviour of continuous learning and intellectual humility (Nadella, 2017). They must cultivate a deep curiosity, openly admit what they do not know, and create a culture where asking questions is a sign of strength. When a leader is comfortable saying, "I don't understand this AI model's output, can you explain it to me?" they create the psychological safety for the entire organisation to learn and adapt.

– From Risk Avoider to Calculated Risk-Taker: The journey to autonomy requires experimentation, and experimentation entails risk. A culture paralysed by a fear of failure will never innovate. The leader's role is to differentiate between reckless gambling and calculated risk-taking. They must create a framework where teams can place smart bets, learn from the outcomes, and even celebrate "intelligent failures" that produce valuable data. For every bold experiment, leaders should require teams to conduct rigorous pre-mortems, identifying potential downsides and designing mitigation strategies in advance.

– From Profit Maximiser to Ethical Steward: Perhaps the most critical shift is the recognition that in the autonomous age, long-term value is inseparable from ethical conduct. As outlined in Chapter 7, the potential for autonomous systems to cause harm through bias or manipulation is immense. The leader must act as the organisation's ultimate ethical steward. This requires moving beyond a narrow focus on short-term profit to prioritise long-term trust and the organisation's social license to operate. When a leader personally chairs a review of a potentially unfair algorithm and chooses to prioritise fairness over immediate profit, as Georgie did, they send a powerful and unforgettable message: progress at this organisation must always align with human values.

This evolution is an ongoing personal journey for any leader, one that requires courage, humility, and the wisdom to lead with questions rather than answers.

Phase 4: Designing for Resilience and Sustainability

No major strategic initiative is without disruptions, setbacks, or unforeseen challenges. Phase 4 is about proactively designing an SDO that can anticipate, withstand, adapt to, and recover from the inevitable failures. As an organisation moves up the SOA, the nature of risk evolves. A Level 1 organisation worries about a human misinterpreting an AI's output; a Level 3 organisation must worry about "automation complacency" and the system's helplessness when faced with a truly novel event, like a sudden supply chain shock, that requires human intervention. Building a robust SDO requires a dual focus on resilience and a broader definition of sustainability.

Designing for Resilience: Building Antifragile Systems

Resilience is more than just disaster recovery; it is about building systems that can absorb shocks and adapt, sometimes even growing stronger from the disruption. This requires embedding the modern operational practices detailed in Chapter 6 into the organisation's DNA. Passively reacting to problems is a losing strategy. Instead, leaders must champion a culture of proactive resilience:

- Embrace Chaos Engineering: This practice, which involves intentionally injecting controlled failures into systems, is a powerful tool for building resilience. Leaders should sponsor and protect "Game Days," where teams simulate system failures – like a key data feed going down or a cloud region becoming unavailable – to test and improve both the system's and the human team's response. The goal is to build confidence that your autonomous systems can handle turbulent conditions before a real-world crisis hits. This moves resilience from a theoretical hope to a tested and proven capability.
- Prioritise Observability: In a complex SDO, you cannot predict every failure mode. Instead of relying on traditional monitoring that only tracks known problems, leaders must invest in observability. This means designing systems that provide deep, real-time insights into their own internal state, allowing teams to rapidly diagnose and resolve novel issues whose root causes are far from obvious. For a leader, this means funding the engineering work required to instrument systems properly and empowering teams with the time and tools to analyse the rich data that observability provides.
- Automate Security and Compliance: Resilience also means being able to withstand security threats and adapt to new regulations. By adopting practices like DevSecOps, security and compliance checks are automated and integrated into the

development pipeline from the very beginning, creating systems that are secure and compliant by design, rather than by audit. This builds a more robust defence against threats and reduces the risk of costly compliance failures.

Designing for Sustainability: A Broader View of Success

In the context of an SDO, sustainability must be defined more broadly than just environmental impact. It is about ensuring the long-term health and viability of the entire human-machine system across four key dimensions. A leader's focus on these four pillars is required for building an organisation that can endure:

- Operational Sustainability: This involves building systems that are maintainable, scalable, and adaptable over the long term. The immediate temptation in the race to automate is to create quick, custom solutions that solve a single problem. This often leads to brittle, overly complex "algorithmic monoliths" that are difficult to understand, expensive to maintain, and impossible to upgrade. Leaders must champion architectural principles like modularity and clear documentation. Operational sustainability means ensuring that the brilliant AI system built today can still be understood, improved, and safely operated by a new team five years from now.

- Financial Sustainability: The journey to autonomy requires significant investment. Financial sustainability means ensuring a demonstrable and ongoing return on these investments. This requires moving beyond the simple, first-order ROI of a pilot project (e.g. "we saved X hours of labour") to continuously tracking the second-order value created across the organisation. This includes measuring the value of increased innovation speed, improved customer retention due to better service, enhanced strategic decision-making, and reduced risk. A financially sustainable SDO is one where the investments in autonomy create a clear and lasting competitive advantage.

- Social Sustainability: This is the ethical commitment to responsibly manage the SDO's impact on people, which is fundamental to maintaining the organisation's social licence to operate. It involves a proactive and sincere investment in reskilling and supporting the workforce through the transition, ensuring that automation is used to augment human capabilities, not just replace them. It means establishing robust governance to promote fairness and mitigate bias in all algorithmic systems. As outlined in the principles of "Progressive Autonomy" from Chapter 5, ensuring that the benefits of increased productivity are shared equitably is not just an ethical ideal; it is an essential strategy for maintaining employee morale, attracting top talent, and building a trusted public brand.

- Environmental Sustainability: SDOs offer a powerful opportunity to move beyond compliance and actively minimise environmental impact, directly contributing to modern ESG (Environmental, Social, and Governance) goals. Leaders can champion "Green AI" initiatives that leverage autonomous systems for tangible benefits. This could involve an AI that manages a building's HVAC and lighting systems in real time based on occupancy to cut energy waste; a system that optimises global logistics routes to reduce fuel consumption and carbon emissions; or a generative AI that designs products using less material without sacrificing strength. In this context, sustainability becomes a source of both efficiency and corporate purpose.

Phase 5: Redefining Performance Measurement

The final phase of the playbook recognises that you cannot navigate a new world with an out-of-date map. Traditional, lagging financial indicators like quarterly profit and revenue, while still important, are insufficient to measure the health and progress of a Self-Driving Organisation. They report on past outcomes but fail to capture the underlying capabilities that drive future success in an autonomous world. Leaders need a new, more balanced scorecard to steer by – a set of new constellations that provide a richer, more holistic view of value creation.

This new scorecard begins by measuring the organisation's very metabolism: its agility and adaptability. In a turbulent environment, the ability to pivot quickly is a primary competitive advantage. An SDO is designed for speed, and its performance measurement must reflect this. Instead of only measuring what was produced, leaders must measure how quickly the organisation can learn and react. This can be captured through metrics such as the average time taken for a critical decision to be made and implemented, the length of innovation cycles from concept to market, and the "time-to-pivot" in response to a major external disruption. This focus on speed, however, must be paired with a focus on quality. A truly agile organisation makes rapid *and* effective decisions, which requires a deep commitment to data.

Therefore, the next layer of the scorecard must track the rate of data-driven decision-making. An SDO runs on data, not just intuition. A basic cultural and operational metric is the extent to which data is actually being used to make choices. Leaders can track the percentage of key strategic and operational decisions that are demonstrably informed by analytics, versus those made primarily by hierarchy or habit. This can be assessed through post-decision audits, which examine the evidence and rationale presented when a decision was made, creating a powerful incentive to ground choices in data. This data-driven approach is the foundation for effective automation.

The impact of this automation effectiveness must also be measured with sophistication. This means moving beyond simple, first-order cost savings to track the deeper value created by automated systems. This includes measuring the reduction in error rates in key processes, the gains in throughput for a production line, and the improvement in customer satisfaction scores from an automated service channel. Critically, it also involves measuring the percentage of employee time that has been successfully shifted from routine, low-value tasks to more creative, high-value work. This directly connects the value of automation to the value of your people.

As automation elevates human talent, the scorecard must reflect the growing value of this human capital. In an SDO, people are the source of innovation, ethical oversight, and strategic direction. Their value can be tracked through employee engagement and satisfaction scores, particularly for those in new AI-augmented roles, and by measuring the development of future-ready skills across the workforce. Leaders should also attempt to measure the innovation contribution – new ideas, patents, or process improvements – from human teams who have been freed from the drudgery of routine tasks, reflecting the core ideas of Chapter 5.

Of course, a highly capable and agile organisation is worthless if it is brittle. The scorecard must therefore incorporate resilience metrics. As discussed in Phase 4, resilience is a designed capability, and it can be measured by monitoring the operational uptime of critical autonomous systems and the Mean Time to Recovery (MTTR) after a failure. Data from proactive resilience testing, such as Chaos Engineering experiments, provides a concrete measure of the organisation's ability to withstand shocks.

Finally, all of these performance dimensions must be wrapped in a layer of ethical performance indicators. Trust is a key asset in the autonomous age, and it must be measured and managed with the same rigour as financial performance. This requires creating metrics to track ethical conduct, such as conducting regular demographic analysis of AI-generated hiring shortlists to audit for fairness, tracking compliance rates with data privacy regulations like GDPR, and using surveys to measure stakeholder and customer trust in the organisation's ethical use of AI, as mandated by the frameworks in Chapter 7.

By adopting this richer, more holistic set of metrics, leaders can foster a new and more accurate understanding of value creation. This new scorecard allows them to manage the organisation based not just on where it has been, but on the capabilities that will determine where it can go.

Summary

The five phases of the playbook are summarised below:
1. **Diagnostic and Strategic Intent:** The process begins with a thorough "autonomy audit" to map the organisation's current position on the Spectrum of Organisational Autonomy (SOA), assessing its technological, cultural, and talent readiness to create a clear, data-driven strategic vision.
2. **Execution Through Pilot Programmes:** The strategy is implemented through a portfolio of carefully selected pilot projects – including quick wins, strategic bets, and seeds of transformation – designed to build momentum, generate organisational learning, and deliver measurable value.

3. **The Evolution of Executive Leadership:** The leader's role must fundamentally shift from a traditional controller to an "architect of intelligent systems." This involves empowering teams, breaking down silos, designing decision-making frameworks, fostering a learning culture, and acting as an ethical steward.

4. **Designing for Resilience and Sustainability:** The organisation must be proactively designed to withstand disruptions by embedding modern operational practices like DevSecOps and Chaos Engineering, while also addressing operational, financial, social, and environmental sustainability.

5. **Redefining Performance Measurement:** Success must be measured with a new, balanced scorecard that goes beyond financial indicators to include metrics for agility, data-driven decision-making, automation effectiveness, resilience, valuing human resources, and ethical performance.

Chapter 10
Conclusion: The Paradoxes of Organisational Autonomy

Our journey across the SOA has reached its destination. We began by reimagining the firm as a self-driving entity, then explored its engine room of AI and blockchain. We ventured to the frontier of governance with DAOs and dissected the SDO's core: its evolving strategic brain, the symbiotic balance of human and machine work, and the new legal and ethical codes required to operate. Finally, after contemplating the emergence of machine leadership, we charted an agenda for navigating this context.

Now, at the end of this exploration, it is time to synthesise these threads, to reflect on their significance for our future. This concluding chapter serves as a point of departure. It is a consideration of the significant emerging power of organisational autonomy and a call for an agenda that considers the responsibility that comes with it. Questions surrounding the SDO have moved from *what* they are to *how* they will be implemented. The answer to that question will be determined by the conscious, deliberate, and often difficult political, economic, and ethical choices we make today, rather than by technological developments alone.

A Synthesis of Tensions: The Foundational Paradoxes of the Autonomous Age

Throughout our analysis, several recurring tensions or paradoxes have emerged. These represent dynamic, dialectical forces that leaders and designers of SDOs must continuously negotiate. Understanding these paradoxes is key to grasping the true nature of the challenge ahead.

First among them is the paradox of control, the necessity of ceding direct control to gain organisational agility. The entire journey across the SOA can be understood as a story of the progressive and deliberate cession of direct, manual, human control. This approach evolves from decades of management theory built on the idea that control is something to be maximised through supervision and hierarchical oversight. Yet, as we have seen, in a world defined by accelerating change, this traditional model of control presents limitations. The SDO embraces a new philosophy. It recognises that in a complex adaptive system, true control – the ability to achieve desired outcomes reliably – comes from designing an intelligent system with a clear purpose and the autonomy to pursue it. The leader's role, as outlined in the playbook in Chapter 9, shifts from being a hands-on controller to becoming an architect of these autonomous systems. This requires a substantial psychological shift and a new comfort level with delegation (Ibarra, 2015). It is by ceding this tactical, direct control that leaders can hope to gain a higher form of strategic control: an organisation that is agile, resilient, and capable of navigating a dynamic world. With this paradox as our guide, we can now examine how decision-making authority is specifically reconfigured at each level of the SOA.

The second great tension is the paradox of humanity, the drive to automate work in order to elevate human contribution. The dominant narrative surrounding autonomy often focuses on replacement. While the disruptive impact on many roles is real, this book has argued for a more considered perspective. The ultimate promise of the SDO is to create more *human-centric* organisations. By systematically automating the tasks that are repetitive and rule-based, we liberate human talent to focus on the work that only humans can do: deep creativity, complex critical thinking, empathy, and robust ethical reasoning. As the socio-technical perspective reminds us, achieving this positive outcome requires deliberate action. The allocation of work is a dynamic social process. Achieving this more humanistic workplace requires a sustained societal investment in "progressive autonomy" – reskilling the workforce, fostering lifelong learning, and designing human–machine interactions that empower and engage the human user.

Third, we have confronted the paradox of governance: the quest for decentralisation and the emergence of new centres of power. One of the most radical promises of the technologies underpinning the SDO, particularly blockchain, is the possibility of creating truly decentralised organisations. The ideal is a flat, democratic landscape of peer-to-peer coordination. Yet, as our exploration of DAO challenges revealed, this quest engages with the practical realities of efficiency and human nature. Purely decentralised voting can be slow, and the "one token, one vote" model often leads to a new form of plutocracy, instead of broader democratic outcomes. In response, we see the emergence of new, more centralised structures – foundations, core development teams, and specialised committees – created to bring efficiency and strategic direction to the decentralised whole. The paradox is that the search for alternative leadership models can lead to the creation of new, less visible, and sometimes less accountable forms of power. This teaches us that designing governance for SDOs is a perpetual balancing act between the competing virtues of decentralisation, efficiency, and autonomy – the organisational trilemma.

Finally, our journey has revealed the paradox of intelligence: the distinction between the smart machine and the wise organisation. We live in an age focused on the "smartness" of our technology. The exponential growth in the capabilities of AI is obviously significant. That said, intelligence – the capacity for computation and pattern matching – is distinct from wisdom. Wisdom is the application of knowledge, experience, and ethical principles to make sound judgements. A smart machine can optimise a supply chain for maximum efficiency. A wise organisation does so while also considering the environmental impact and the well-being of its workers. A smart machine can personalise marketing with unerring accuracy. A wise organisation, as we discussed in our exploration of autonomous influence, knows when personalisation crosses the line into manipulation and erodes customer trust. This wisdom must be supplied by human leadership and deliberately embedded into the organisation's culture, its governance structures, and its ethical frameworks. The paradox is that the more intelligent our machines become, the more critical our own human wisdom becomes in guiding them.

A Shared Voyage: The Call for Conscious, Collaborative Shaping

If these paradoxes teach us anything, it is that the future of the SDO is a design space with many possible outcomes. How it all pans out will be the result of the countless choices made by leaders, technologists, policymakers, and society at large. The autonomous future, therefore, is a collective endeavour that requires our active and conscious shaping and recognition of the different stakes, and voices, that we all have in it.

This demands a new politics of technology and a commitment to multi-stakeholder dialogue. This book is intended as a modest contribution to such politics and a call to decision-makers at every level in organisations to engage in it, practically and philosophically. It is a call to move from being controllers to being architects, from silo guardians to network weavers, and from profit maximisers to ethical stewards. It is a call to technologists to embrace a new ethos of responsible innovation, asking not just "can we build it?" but "should we build it?" And it is a call to policymakers to embrace more agile and collaborative approaches that can keep pace with technology, protecting citizens while enabling innovation and economic development.

The SDO, in its final, fully realised form, may still be just beyond our current capacity to build but it is certainly not beyond our imagination. Every great transformation begins as an idea that stretches the bounds of the possible. The traverse of the SOA is already well underway in our institutions and organisations, sometimes in an obvious, planned deliberate way, sometimes in haphazard, reactionary and opportunistic ways, and sometimes through insidious, almost invisible means. The SDO represents the azimuth on this journey of discovery, learning, and adaptation. The challenges are formidable, and the potential benefits – organisations that are more agile, more resilient, more innovative, and ultimately more capable of addressing the complex problems of our time – are significant. We are actively creating the future, one decision, one algorithm, and one organisation at a time. We need to proceed with our eyes open, and all of our other senses fully alert too.

Appendix 1: The Spectrum of Organisational Autonomy (SOA) Diagnostic Tool

Introduction and Instructions

This diagnostic tool is a companion to the book, *The Spectrum of Organisational Autonomy*. It is designed for executives, strategists, and leaders to conduct a thorough "autonomy audit" of their organisation or specific functional units.

The purpose is not to achieve the highest possible score, but to create an honest, data-rich map of your organisation's current reality. This allows you to consciously and deliberately make strategic choices about the right level of autonomy for your specific context.

How to Use This Tool:

1. **Assemble a Cross-Functional Team:** For the most accurate assessment, convene a group of leaders from key areas such as strategy, operations, IT, HR, finance, and legal.
2. **Assess Function by Function:** The SOA is not a single ladder every part of the organisation climbs in unison. It is common for a company to exhibit characteristics from multiple levels simultaneously across different departments. Assess each functional area independently.
3. **Select the "Best Fit":** For each question, read all the descriptions and select the one that most accurately reflects the *current state* of your organisation or unit. Be unflinchingly honest.
4. **Synthesise and Analyse:** Use the "Interpreting Your Results" section to create your organisation's "Autonomy Profile" and discuss the strategic implications.

Part 1: Overall Autonomy Snapshot

To begin, read the summary descriptions of the six SOA levels below. Based on your initial "gut feel" and holistic view of your organisation, which level best describes your company's dominant operational logic today?

- **Level 0: Human-Centric Governance**
  - Human actors exercise complete control and are responsible for all operations. Machines are passive instruments, subservient to human intent. Decision-making authority resides entirely within the human element.
- **Level 1: Assisted Autonomy**
  - Humans remain firmly in command but are substantively assisted by technology that provides data-driven insights and automates routine information gathering. Technology enhances but does not replace human judgment.

© 2026 Walter de Gruyter GmbH, Berlin | https://doi.org/10.1515/9783112222232-012

- **Level 2: Partial Autonomy**
  - The system can autonomously handle specific, well-defined tasks under pre-programmed conditions. Human oversight is readily available and frequently required for managing exceptions and complex scenarios.
- **Level 3: Conditional Autonomy**
  - Machines and algorithms autonomously manage substantial, complex processes under normal circumstances. Human intervention is necessary, but primarily for addressing novel or exceptional situations outside the system's design parameters.
- **Level 4: High Autonomy and Collaborative Intelligence**
  - The system autonomously handles almost all operational and tactical decisions. Human involvement shifts fundamentally to strategic guidance, ethical oversight, setting goals, and managing novel crises. This is the level mature DAOs may begin to align with.
- **Level 5: Full Autonomy / Autonomous Evolution (Theoretical)**
  - The system is capable of handling all aspects of its operation in any environment without human involvement. It can independently learn, adapt, and set its own operational and strategic goals. This level is currently speculative for conventional organisations.

Our Organisation's Overall Estimated Level: ____

Part 2: Detailed Functional Assessment

For each of the following seven domains, select the statement that best describes your organisation or business unit.

Domain 1: Strategy, Planning, and Decision-Making

- **Level 0:** Strategy is a top-down, episodic, and deliberative affair, conceived through human cognition, debate, and experience-based frameworks (e.g. SWOT, Porter's Five Forces). All significant decisions are centralised in human leaders.
- **Level 1:** Human leaders retain full control of strategy, but their judgment is augmented by AI-powered tools that provide sophisticated forecasts, competitor analyses, and market insights. The AI influences decisions, but humans make the final call.
- **Level 2:** Strategy is centrally defined, but its tactical execution is decentralised to empowered teams who operate within predefined strategic boundaries (e.g. using OKRs). AI tools provide real-time performance feedback to support team-level decisions.

- **Level 3:** AI begins to autonomously shape and execute strategy in specific domains (e.g. dynamic pricing, network optimisation). Planning becomes a continuous, adaptive process driven by real-time data. Human strategists shift to designing and overseeing these autonomous systems.
- **Level 4:** Humans and AI engage in a creative collaboration on developing strategy. AI acts as a generative partner, proposing novel options, modelling complex scenarios, and identifying emergent opportunities that humans then validate, guide, and ethically approve.
- **Level 5 (Theoretical):** The AI system autonomously defines its own strategic goals and adapts its long-term trajectory with minimal or no human intervention, raising questions of purpose and control.

Our Score for this Domain: _____

Domain 2: Allocation of Work and Human-Machine Collaboration

- **Level 0:** Humans perform nearly all tasks, from high-level strategy to granular manual labour. Expertise is embodied entirely in people and their tacit knowledge. Machines are simple, passive tools.
- **Level 1:** Humans retain control over core processes but use technology for enhanced insights and automation of routine information gathering. The goal is augmentation: making the human expert faster and better informed.
- **Level 2:** Specific, well-defined tasks are handed over to machines (e.g. RPA bots, simple chatbots). Humans manage by exception, handling complex edge cases and scenarios requiring judgment that falls outside the automated system's capabilities.
- **Level 3:** Machines autonomously manage substantial operational processes. The human role transitions decisively to higher-level oversight: designing, tuning, and guarding the autonomous systems and intervening in novel or exceptional situations.
- **Level 4:** A true symbiotic partnership emerges where humans and AI co-create value. Humans focus on purpose, ethical frameworks, and creative direction in collaboration with AI, which handles operations and performs complex analysis.
- **Level 5 (Theoretical):** The traditional concept of work allocation is moot as the system manages all operational aspects. Human involvement may be limited to initial creation, setting ultimate ethical backstops, or being beneficiaries of the system.

Our Score for this Domain: _____

Domain 3: Governance and Organisational Structure

- **Level 0/1:** The organisation relies on traditional hierarchical governance structures with clear reporting lines and centralised control in boards and executive committees.
- **Level 2:** Hierarchical structures begin to flatten or become more matrix-like and networked. Agile approaches are prevalent, empowering teams with greater operational autonomy within defined frameworks.
- **Level 3:** We see the emergence of early forms of "algorithmic governance" (ALGov) where operational rules are encoded into software. Humans oversee these systems and manage by exception.
- **Level 4:** Algorithmic governance is mature. In DAOs, governance is executed by smart contracts and token-holder voting. In traditional firms, AI systems may handle vast operational decisions, with humans focusing on ethical governance and strategic direction in a collaborative authority structure.
- **Level 5 (Theoretical):** Governance is fully executed by code, with the system capable of complete self-governance and even modifying its own rules based on learning and adaptation. The question of legal personhood for the AI becomes a central issue.

Our Score for this Domain: _____

Domain 4: Ethics and Accountability

- **Level 0/1:** Ethical concerns focus on traditional human bias and established legal compliance. Accountability lines are generally clear and point to identifiable human decision-makers.
- **Level 2:** The "problem of many hands" begins to emerge, where accountability for an automated error is difficult to assign to a single actor. Concerns about bias being encoded in rule-based systems appear.
- **Level 3:** The "accountability vacuum" becomes a significant challenge (e.g. who is liable for an autonomous vehicle crash?). The "black box" nature of AI poses a challenge to transparency and trust.
- **Level 4:** In DAOs, the lack of legal personality creates immense accountability challenges, with members potentially facing unlimited personal liability. In corporations, there is a formal, proactive approach to ethics, including bias audits, XAI implementation, ethics boards, and diverse development teams.
- **Level 5 (Theoretical):** The "AI control problem" is the central ethical challenge: ensuring that a self-evolving, potentially superintelligent system remains aligned with human values.

Our Score for this Domain: _____

Domain 5: Leadership and Management Philosophy

- **Level 0/1/2:** Leadership is a human-centric activity. At lower levels, it is based on "command and control." As teams become more empowered, it shifts towards facilitation and creating the right environment for success, using frameworks like Agile and Lean.
- **Level 3:** "Algorithmic Management" emerges in specific sectors, where AI systems assign tasks, monitor performance, and provide feedback. Human leadership focuses on designing and overseeing these systems.
- **Level 4:** "Machine Leadership" becomes more pronounced, with the AI acting as a recognised decision authority or the DAO protocol itself acting as the leader. Human leaders evolve into architects of purpose, ethical stewards, and orchestrators of human-AI collaboration.
- **Level 5 (Theoretical):** Machine leadership is absolute. An AGI would define the organisation's purpose and direct its own evolution, marking the transition from humans leading machines to being led by them.

Our Score for this Domain: ____

Domain 6: Legal, Compliance, and Security

- **Level 0/1:** The landscape is familiar, governed by established employment, contract, and tort law. Security concerns are traditional (e.g. network security, access control).
- **Level 2:** New legal questions arise around IP ownership of AI-assisted creations and liability for biased algorithmic recommendations. Security focuses on protecting the data used by these fledgling AI tools.
- **Level 3:** Legal frameworks begin to fracture, with intense debate around liability for autonomous systems (e.g. AVs) and the enforceability of flawed smart contracts. Security risks expand to include data poisoning and adversarial attacks on AI models.
- **Level 4:** The legal status of DAOs is a critical unresolved issue globally. Security is paramount, with a focus on smart contract security audits, IoT vulnerabilities, and protecting against governance attacks on DAOs. Modern practices like DevSecOps and Chaos Engineering are adopted.
- **Level 5 (Theoretical):** Existing legal frameworks are entirely inadequate. Fundamental concepts like legal personhood, control, and accountability for superintelligent AI would need to be invented.

Our Score for This Domain: ____

Domain 7: Foundational Technology Readiness

(This is a checklist rather than a scored level)

Review your organisation's capabilities against the core enabling technologies described in Chapter 2. Check all that apply.

- **Artificial Intelligence (AI) and Machine Learning (ML):**
    - [] We have dedicated data science talent and use AI/ML for analytics that *inform* human decisions.
    - [] We have deployed AI/ML models that *autonomously execute* specific tasks (e.g. fraud detection, predictive maintenance).
    - [] We have mature MLOps practices for the reliable deployment and monitoring of ML models.
- **Automation:**
    - [] We use Robotic Process Automation (RPA) to automate repetitive, rule-based digital tasks.
    - [] We use Intelligent Automation (IA), combining RPA with AI (e.g. NLP, OCR), to handle semi-structured tasks.
- **Distributed Ledger Technology:**
    - [] We are experimenting with blockchain for supply chain transparency or record-keeping.
    - [] We use smart contracts to automate multi-party agreements or governance processes.
- **Internet of Things (IoT):**
    - [] We use IoT sensors to gather real-time data from our physical operations.
    - [] Our IoT devices act as effectors, executing physical actions based on AI-driven decisions.
- **Infrastructure and Practices:**
    - [] We have a modern data infrastructure (e.g. data lake) and strong data governance policies.
    - [] We have a mature API strategy that allows our systems to connect and communicate effectively.
    - [] We have adopted modern operational practices like DevOps, Observability, and/or Chaos Engineering.

Part 3: Interpreting Your Results – Your Organisational Autonomy Profile

1. **Create Your Profile:** Plot your scores (0–5) for Domains 1–6 on the radar chart below. Connect the dots to create your organisation's unique "SOA Fingerprint."
   (A blank radar chart with 6 axes, labelled with the domain names, would be inserted here for the user to fill out.)

2. **Analyse the Shape:**
   - **Is your profile balanced and circular?** A consistently low score (e.g. all 1s and 2s) indicates a traditional organisation that may be vulnerable to disruption but has clear, understandable processes. A consistently high score (e.g. all 4s) indicates a highly mature SDO, but one that is exposed to the most complex legal, ethical, and security risks.
   - **Is your profile "spiky"?** This is the most common result. A spike in one area (e.g. Level 3 in Operations) with low scores elsewhere (e.g. Level 1 in HR and Legal) highlights uneven development. This can create internal friction, integration challenges, and situations where your technology has outpaced your governance and talent.
   - **Where are the biggest gaps?** Compare your profile to your strategic ambitions. If your goal is a Level 4 collaborative R&D function, but your "Allocation of Work" and "Leadership" scores are at Level 1, you have identified a critical gap in culture and capabilities that must be addressed.
3. **Reflect and Discuss:** Use these questions to guide a strategic conversation with your team:
   - Where is our current lack of autonomy causing the most friction, cost, or risk?
   - Where are the "quick win" opportunities to pilot greater autonomy and build momentum?
   - Are our technology capabilities (Domain 7) sufficient to support our ambitions? Where are the foundational gaps in our infrastructure or data governance?
   - Is our culture – particularly our attitude towards risk, experimentation, and data-driven decision-making – an enabler or an obstacle?
   - Have we fully anticipated and considered the legal, ethical, and accountability challenges that come with higher levels of autonomy?

Part 4: Next Steps – Applying the Executive Playbook

This diagnostic is the first step in the "Voyage of Discovery" outlined in Chapter 9. Your Autonomy Profile provides the data-driven map of your starting point. Use these results to inform the next phases of your journey:
- **Phase 2: The Ascent:** Identify the most promising pilot projects based on your analysis of pain points and opportunities.
- **Phase 3: New Leadership:** Use the insights on leadership and culture to begin the necessary transformation of your own and your team's leadership style.
- **Phase 4: Riding Out the Storms:** Use the security and legal assessments to proactively design for resilience and sustainability.

- **Phase 5: New Constellations to Steer By:** Develop a new, richer scorecard to measure success in a way that goes beyond traditional financial metrics to include agility, resilience, and ethical performance.

The journey to an SDO is a transformative mission. With this diagnostic in hand, you are now equipped to lead it with greater clarity, purpose, and strategic foresight. Good luck!

Glossary of Terms

Algorithmic Governance (ALGov)
The use of software, often in the form of smart contracts, to encode and execute an organisation's operational rules, decision-making processes, and resource allocation mechanisms. This form of governance, where code plays a central role in enforcement, is a key feature of organisations at higher levels of the Spectrum of Organisational Autonomy, particularly DAOs.

Artificial Intelligence (AI)
A broad field of computer science focused on enabling machines to emulate aspects of human intelligence, such as complex problem-solving, learning from experience, and sophisticated decision-making. In the context of the SDO, AI and its subfield, Machine Learning, function as the "distributed cognitive engine" that allows the organisation to perceive its environment, learn from data, and optimise its actions.

Automation
The use of systems to perform rigid, predictable, and often repetitive functions, typically under a degree of human oversight where performance can be easily verified. It is distinct from autonomy, as it focuses on executing predefined tasks rather than making adaptive decisions in complex environments.

Autonomy
In the organisational context, the capacity of the organisation as an integrated system to function, make decisions, and adapt with significantly reduced direct human operational involvement. It implies a deeper level of independence than automation, where a system is trusted to manage unforeseen circumstances and make adaptive decisions based on goals, often involving a deliberate cession of control by humans.

Blockchain
A shared, cryptographically secured, and distributed digital ledger that is virtually impossible to tamper with. It provides a transparent and immutable infrastructure for recording transactions and enforcing rules, removing the need for a central intermediary and serving as a foundational technology for DAOs and other decentralised systems.

Chaos Engineering
The practice of proactively and intentionally injecting controlled failures into a system to observe how it responds, identify weaknesses, and build more resilient and fault-tolerant autonomous systems before real-world failures can cause disruption.

"Code is Law"
A foundational mantra within the DAO ecosystem signifying the intention for the rules embedded in smart contracts to directly and automatically govern an organisation's behaviour. This minimises the need for human interpretation, intermediation, or external enforcement. The concept was challenged by the hack of "The DAO," which demonstrated that flawed code could lead to catastrophic outcomes.

The Control Problem (AI Alignment)
The challenge of ensuring that highly autonomous or superintelligent AI systems (characteristic of SOA Levels 4 and 5) remain aligned with human intentions and values to avoid causing unintended, catastrophic harm. It addresses the risk of an AI pursuing a poorly specified goal with ruthless efficiency, leading to unforeseen negative consequences.

Decentralised Autonomous Organisation (DAO)
An organisation whose operational logic, financial transactions, and governance records are predominantly encoded on a blockchain and executed by self-enforcing smart contracts. DAOs aim for

decentralised control distributed among their members or token holders, often prioritising governance autonomy over the operational autonomy sought by traditional corporations. They are considered to be at the "vanguard" of organisational autonomy.

DevOps

A cultural and professional movement that emphasises collaboration and communication between software development (Dev) and IT operations (Ops) teams, combined with the automation of infrastructure and deployment processes to enable faster and more reliable updates to systems.

Explainable AI (XAI)

A field of AI focused on developing techniques to make the decisions and predictions of AI models, particularly complex "black box" systems, more understandable to humans. XAI is needed for building trust, detecting algorithmic bias, and establishing accountability in autonomous systems.

GitOps

An operational practice that extends DevOps by using the Git version control system as the single source of truth for managing both application code and infrastructure configurations. This enhances consistency, traceability, and auditability in complex systems.

Governance Token

A type of cryptographic token, unique to a specific DAO, that grants its holders certain rights and privileges, most commonly voting power on proposals concerning the organisation's governance and treasury.

Intelligent Automation (IA)/Cognitive Automation

The convergence of Robotic Process Automation (RPA) with AI capabilities such as machine learning and natural language processing (NLP). IA can handle more complex and semi-structured tasks that require a degree of judgement or interpretation beyond the scope of simple RPA.

Internet of Things (IoT)

The vast, interconnected network of physical devices – such as sensors and actuators embedded in machinery, vehicles, and buildings – that collect, transmit, and act upon data from the physical world. In an SDO, IoT devices serve as the "sensory apparatus and actuation limbs," bridging the digital and physical realms.

Machine Leadership

A phenomenon, emerging at higher levels of the SOA, where a non-human entity (such as an AI, an algorithmic management system, or a DAO protocol) holds and exercises directive capacity, making decisions and coordinating actions previously confined to human leaders.

Machine Learning (ML)

A critical subset of AI that empowers systems to learn from data and improve their performance over time without being explicitly programmed for every scenario (Jordan and Mitchell, 2015). By identifying patterns and making statistical inferences, ML algorithms can adapt and enhance their efficacy, forming the learning component of an SDO's cognitive engine.

MLOps (Machine Learning Operations)

A specialised discipline that combines machine learning best practices with DevOps principles to streamline and standardise the process of building, deploying, and maintaining ML models in production environments.

Observability
The practice of designing systems to provide deep, real-time insights into their internal state through detailed logs, metrics, and traces. It goes beyond traditional monitoring to allow teams to quickly diagnose and resolve issues in complex, distributed autonomous systems.

The Organisational Trilemma
A foundational concept positing that the three desirable organisational goals of autonomy (self-government), decentralisation (distributed control), and efficiency (optimising resources) are often in conflict, requiring strategic trade-offs. An organisation typically cannot maximise all three simultaneously.

Organisational Autonomy
See *Autonomy.*

Progressive Autonomy
A framework advocating for a staged, deliberate, and human-centric transition towards more autonomous systems. It emphasises a societal and organisational commitment to reskilling the workforce, focusing on augmenting human capabilities rather than simple replacement, proactive change management, and prioritising ethical considerations.

Robotic Process Automation (RPA)
Software "bots" designed to mimic human actions to perform repetitive, rule-based digital tasks within existing software applications, such as logging into systems, copying and pasting data, and filling out forms.

Self-Driving Organisation (SDO)
An organisation architected to learn, adapt, and evolve its core operational processes and decision-making frameworks with significantly reduced direct human intervention. The "self-driving promise" is to generate step-changes in organisational agility, efficiency, resilience, and innovation.

Smart Contract
Self-executing contracts where the terms of an agreement are written directly into lines of code that reside on a blockchain. They automatically execute predefined actions when specific, verifiable conditions are met, forming the operational and governance core of DAOs.

Spectrum of Organisational Autonomy (SOA)
A novel conceptual framework introduced in this book that charts six distinct levels of self-governance, from Level 0 (fully human-led) to the theoretical Level 5 (fully autonomous). It serves as an analytical tool to understand the journey, trade-offs, and possibilities at each stage of organisational autonomy.

Bibliography

Adadi, A. and Berrada, M. (2018). Peeking inside the black-box: A survey on Explainable Artificial Intelligence (XAI). In: *IEEE Access*, 6, 52138–52160.

Agrawal, A., Gans, J. and Goldfarb, A. (2018). *Prediction Machines: The Simple Economics of Artificial Intelligence*. Harvard Business Press.

Akella, P., Bikhchandani, P. and Tchakatumba, D. (2020). *The Rise of the Cobot: How Next-gen Robots are Transforming Manufacturing. McKinsey and Company*.

Autor, D. H. (2015). Why are there still so many jobs? The history and future of workplace automation. *Journal of Economic Perspectives*, 29(3), 3–30.

Automation Anywhere. (2023). *Agentic Process Automation: Ushering in the Next Wave of Business Automation*. [White Paper].

Bacharach, M. (2005). "Foreword: Teamwork". *Gold, Teamwork Multi-Disciplinary Perspectives, Palgrave Macmillan*, xxi–xxv.

Bainbridge, L. (1983). Ironies of automation. *Automatica*, 19(6), 775–779.

Banks, I. M. (1987). *Consider Phlebas*. Macmillan.

Banks, I. M. (1988). *The Player of Games*. Macmillan.

Banks, I. M. (1996). *Excession*. Orbit.

Barley, S. R. (1986). Technology as an occasion for structuring: Evidence from observations of ct scanners and the social order of radiology departments. *Administrative Science Quarterly*, 31(1), 78–108.

Barley, S. R. (2020). *Work and Technological Change. Clarendon Lectures in Management Studies*. Oxford University Press.

Barocas, S. and Selbst, A. D. (2016). Big data's disparate impact. *California Law Review*, 104, 671–732.

Bostrom, N. (2014). *Superintelligence: Paths, Dangers, Strategies*. Oxford University Press.

Bradshaw, J. M., Hoffman, R. R., Johnson, M. and Woods, D. D. (2013). The seven deadly myths of "autonomous systems". *IEEE Intelligent Systems*, 28(3), 54–61.

Brown, C. (2007). Utopias and heterotopias: The 'Culture' of Iain M. Banks. *Utopianism/Literary Utopias and National Cultural Identities: A Comparative Perspective*, 249–257.

Buterin, V. (2014). A next-generation smart contract and decentralised application platform. [White paper].

Buterin, V. (2017). The Blockchain Scalability Trilemma. [Blog post].

Calo, R. (2015). Robotics and the lessons of cyberlaw. *California Law Review*, 103, 513–563.

Casey, M. J. and Wong, P. (2017, March 13). Global supply chains are about to get better, thanks to blockchain. *Harvard Business Review*.

Chalmers, D. J. (1996). *The Conscious Mind: In Search of a Fundamental Theory*. Oxford University Press.

Cherns, A. (1976). The principles of sociotechnical design. *Human Relations*, 29(8), 783–792.

Chitra, T. (2021, November 18). Why are DAOs the future of work?. *Andreessen Horowitz (A16z) Crypto Blog*.

Chopra, S. and White, L. F. (2011). *A Legal Theory for Autonomous Artificial Agents*. University of Michigan Press.

ConstitutionDAO. (n.d). We're buying the US Constitution. [Archived website].

Danaher, J. (2016). The threat of algocracy: Reality, resistance and accommodation. *Philosophy and Technology*, 29(3), 245–268.

Dastin, J. (2018, October 10). Amazon scraps secret AI recruiting tool that showed bias against women. *Reuters*.

Daugherty, P. R., and Wilson, H. J. (2018). *Human+ Machine: Reimagining Work in the Age of AI*. Harvard Business Press.

Dennett, D. C. (1987). *The Intentional Stance*. MIT press.

DuPont, Q. (2017). Experiments in algorithmic governance: A history and ethnography of "The DAO," a failed decentralised autonomous organisation. In: *Bitcoin and Beyond*, Routledge, 157–177.

Endsley, M. R. (2017). From here to autonomy: Lessons learned from human-automation research. *Human Factors*, 59(1), 5–27.

Eubanks, V. (2018). *Automating Inequality: How High-tech Tools Profile, Police, and Punish the Poor*. St. Martin's Press.

Ferreira, D. and Li, J. (2021). *The organisational trilemma*. [Unpublished working paper].

Floridi, L., and Sanders, J. W. (2004). On the morality of artificial agents. *Minds and Machines*, 14(3), 349–379.

Galbraith, J. R. (2002). *Designing Organisations: An Executive Guide to Strategy, Structure, and Process*. Jossey-Bass.

Gans, J. and Goldfarb, A. (2023). Could an AI run your company?. *Harvard Business Review*.

Gault, M. (2021, November 19). *Why ConstitutionDAO Lost the Auction*. Vice.

The GitOps Working Group. (n.d.). *OpenGitOps Principles*. Retrieved from opengitops.dev

Ghoshal, S. and Moran, P. (1996). Bad for practice: A critique of the transaction cost theory. *Academy of Management Review*, 21(1), 13–47.

Glikson, E., and Woolley, A. W. (2020). Human trust in artificial intelligence: A multidisciplinary review and research agenda. *The Academy of Management Annals*, 14(2), 627–660.

Goodman, B. and Flaxman, S. (2017). European Union regulations on algorithmic decision-making and a "right to explanation". *AI Magazine*, 38(3), 50–57.

Gubbi, J., Buyya, R., Marusic, S. and Palaniswami, M. (2013). Internet of Things (IoT): A vision, architectural elements, and future directions. *Future Generation Computer Systems*, 29(7), 1645–1660.

Gunning, D. and Aha, D. (2019). DARPA's Explainable Artificial Intelligence (XAI) Program. *AI Magazine*, 40(2), 44–58.

Haraway, D. J. (1991). *Simians, Cyborgs, and Women: The Reinvention of Nature*. New York: Routledge.

Holstein, K., Vaughan, J. W., Daumé III, H., Dudik, M., and Wallach, H. (2019). Improving fairness in machine learning systems: What do industry practitioners need?. In: *Proceedings of the 2019 CHI Conference on Human Factors in Computing Systems*.

Hsieh, Y.-Y., and Vergne, J. P. (2023). The future of the web? The paradoxes and promises of decentralised autonomous organisations (DAOs). In: *Research Handbook on Digital Transformation*, Edward Elgar Publishing.

Ibarra, H. (2015). The authenticity paradox. *Harvard Business Review*, 93(1/2), 52–59.

Jarrahi, M. H. (2018). Artificial intelligence and the future of work: Human-AI symbiosis in organisational decision making. *Business Horizons*, 61(4), 577–586.

Jordan, M. I. and Mitchell, T. M. (2015). Machine learning: Trends, perspectives, and prospects. *Science*, 349(6245), 255–260.

Kagermann, H., Wahlster, W., and Helbig, J. (2013). *Recommendations for Implementing the Strategic Initiative INDUSTRIE 4.0*.

Kamilaris, A., Fonts, A. and Prenafeta-Boldú, F. X. (2019). The rise of blockchain technology in agriculture and food supply chains. *Trends in Food Science and Technology*, 91, 640–652.

Keep, E. and Mayhew, K. (1999). The assessment: knowledge, skills, and competitiveness. *Oxford Review of Economic Policy*, 15(1), 1–15.

Kim, G., Humble, J., Debois, P. and Willis, J. (2016). *The DevOps Handbook: How to Create World-class Agility, Reliability, and Security in Technology Organisations*. IT Revolution Press.

Klein, E. (2021, December 3). *The Loneliness of the Digital Native. The New York Times*.

Lee, I. and Lee, K. (2015). The Internet of Things (IoT): Applications, investments, and challenges for enterprises. *Business Horizons*, 58(4), 431–440.

Lee, M. K., Kusbit, D., Metsky, E. and Dabbish, L. (2015). Working with machines: The impact of algorithmic and data-driven management on human workers. In: *Proceedings of the 33rd Annual ACM Conference on Human Factors in Computing Systems*.

Lessig, L. (1999). *Code and Other Laws of Cyberspace*. Basic books.

London, A. J. (2019). Artificial intelligence and black-box medical decisions: Accuracy versus explainability. *The Hastings Center Report*, 49(1), 15–21.

MakerDAO. (n.d). *MakerDAO: An Unbiased Global Financial System*. White Paper.

MakerDAO. (2022). *Legal and Risk Analysis of RWA. MakerDAO Forum*.

Mateescu, A. and Nguyen, A. (2019). *Algorithmic Management in the Workplace*. Data and Society.

Matthias, A. (2004). The responsibility gap: Ascribing responsibility for the actions of learning automata. *Ethics and Information Technology*, 6(3), 175–183.

McAfee, A., and Brynjolfsson, E. (2017). *Machine, Platform, Crowd: Harnessing Our Digital Future*. W. W. Norton and Company.

Mendlesohn, F. (2003). Iain M. Banks: The Culture. In: *A Companion to Science Fiction*, Blackwell Publishing, 565–570.

Metz, C. (2023, March 23). *The AI Revolution Will Change the Way We Create Art. The New York Times*.

Meyerson, D., Weick, K. E. and Kramer, R. M. (1996). "Swift trust and temporary groups". In: Kramer, R. M. and Tyler, T. R. (Eds.). *Trust in Organisations: Frontiers of Theory and Research*, Thousand Oaks, CA: Sage Publications, 166–195.

Mintzberg, H. (1994). The fall and rise of strategic planning. *Harvard Business Review*, 72(1), 107–114.

Nadella, S. (2017). *Hit Refresh: The Quest to Rediscover Microsoft's Soul and Imagine a Better Future for Everyone*. HarperCollins.

Ngai, E. W. T., Hu, Y., Wong, Y. H., Chen, Y., and Sun, X. (2011). The application of data mining techniques in financial fraud detection: A classification framework and an academic review of the literature. *Decision Support Systems*, 50(3), 559–569.

Nissenbaum, H. (1996). Accountability in a computerised society. *Science and Engineering Ethics*, 2(1), 25–42.

Noble, S. U. (2018). *Algorithms of Oppression: How Search Engines Reinforce Racism*. NYU Press.

O'Keefe, T. (2016). 'A Sign of the Future': The Utopian Future of Post-Scarcity in Iain M. *Banks' Culture Series. Utopian Studies*, 27(2), 268–286.

O'Neil, C. (2016). *Weapons of Math Destruction: How Big Data Increases Inequality and Threatens Democracy*. Broadway Books.

Orlikowski, W. J. (1992). The duality of technology: rethinking the concept of technology in organisations. *Organisation Science*, 3(3), 398–427.

Palmer, C. (2014). 'Beautiful and impossible': The utopian philosophy of Iain M. *Banks' Culture. Open Library of Humanities*, 1(1).

Parasuraman, R., Sheridan, T. B. and Wickens, C. D. (2000). A model for types and levels of human interaction with automation. *IEEE Transactions on Systems, Man, and cybernetics-Part A: Systems and Humans*, 30(3), 286–297.

Parmy, O. (2021, November 19). A crypto bid to buy a copy of the US Constitution goes sideways. *Bloomberg*.

Pasmore, W. A. (1995). Social science transformed: The socio-technical perspective. *Human Relations*, 48(1), 1–21.

Pasquale, F. (2015). *The Black Box Society: The Secret Algorithms that Control Money and Information*. Harvard University Press.

Porter, M. E. and Heppelmann, J. E. (2014). How smart, connected products are transforming competition. *Harvard Business Review*, 92(11), 64–88.

Poursabzi-Sangdeh, F., ..., Vaughan, J. W., and Wallach, H. (2021). Manipulating and measuring model interpretability. In: *Proceedings of the 2021 CHI Conference on Human Factors in Computing Systems*.

Price, W. N., and Cohen, I. G. (2019). Privacy in the age of medical big data. *Nature Medicine*, 25(1), 37–43.

Proffitt, B. (2021). *The State of the DAOs*.

Radchenko, A. (2021, August 11). What is GitOps?. *Weaveworks Blog*.

Raisch, S. and Krakowski, S. (2021). Artificial intelligence and management: The automation–augmentation paradox. *Academy of Management Review*, 46(1), 192–210.

Rogers, D. L. (2016). *The Digital Transformation Playbook: Rethink Your Business for the Digital Age*. Columbia University Press.

Roose, K. (2022, September 2). An A.I.-generated picture won an art prize. In: *Artists Aren't Happy, The New York Times*.

Rosenblat, A. (2018). *Uberland: How Algorithms Are Rewriting the Rules of Work*. University of California Press.

Rudin, C. (2019). Stop explaining black box machine learning models for high stakes decisions and use interpretable models instead. *Nature Machine Intelligence*, 1(5), 206–215.

Russell, S. (2019). *Human Compatible: Artificial Intelligence and the Problem of Control*. Viking.

Schein, E. H. (2010). *Organisational Culture and Leadership* (2nd ed.). John Wiley and Sons.

Schneider, S. (2009). The utopian robotics of Iain M. Banks's Culture series. *Extrapolation*, 50(2), 298–315.

Schwab, K. (2017). *The Fourth Industrial Revolution*. Crown Business.

Searle, J. R. (1980). Minds, brains, and programs. *Behavioral and Brain Sciences*, 3(3), 417–424.

Shrestha, Y. R., Ben-Menahem, S. M., and Von Krogh, G. (2019). Organisational decision-making structures in the age of artificial intelligence. *California Management Review*, 61(4), 66–83.

Siegel, D. (2016, June 25). Understanding The DAO attack. *CoinDesk*.

Smith, B. C. (2019). The promise of artificial intelligence. In: *The Oxford Handbook of Ethics of AI*, Oxford University Press.

Szabo, N. (1997). The idea of smart contracts. *Nick Szabo's Essays, Papers, and Concise Tutorials*.

Tapscott, D. and Tapscott, A. (2018). *Blockchain Revolution: How the Technology behind Bitcoin Is Changing Money, Business, and the World*. Portfolio/Penguin.

Trist, E. L., and Bamforth, K. W. (1951). Some social and psychological consequences of the Longwall method of coal-getting. *Human Relations*, 4(1), 3–38.

Tushman, M. L. and O'Reilly, C. A., III. (2002). *Winning through Innovation: A Practical Guide to Leading Organisational Change and Renewal*. Harvard Business Press.

Uniswap. (n.d.). *Uniswap Protocol*. Retrieved from uniswap.org

Uniswap Foundation. (2023). A proposal to create the Uniswap Foundation. *Uniswap Governance Forum*.

Vincent, J. (2023, April 17). AI-generated music is here, and the world is not ready. *The Verge*.

Wachter, S., Mittelstadt, B. and Floridi, L. (2017). Why a right to explanation of automated decision-making does not exist in the General Data Protection Regulation. *International Data Privacy Law*, 7(2), 76–99.

Walch, A. (2019). Deconstructing 'Decentralisation': Exploring the core claim of crypto systems. In: *Cryptoassets: Legal, Regulatory, and Monetary Perspectives*, Oxford University Press.

Waters, R. (2016, June 18). 'The DAO' hack and the future of blockchain. *Financial Times*.

Wenger, E. (1998). *Communities of Practice – Learning, Meaning and Identity*. Cambridge University Press.

Westerman, G., Bonnet, D. and McAfee, A. (2014). *Leading Digital: Turning Technology into Business Transformation*. Harvard Business Press.

Westerman, G., Soule, D. L. and Eswaran, A. (2019). *Designed for Digital: How to Architect Your Business for Sustained Success*. MIT Press.

Wright, A. and De Filippi, P. (2015). Decentralised blockchain technology and the rise of Lex Cryptographia. *SSRN Electronic Journal*.

Yeung, K. (2018). Algorithmic regulation: A critical interrogation. *Regulation and Governance*, 12(4), 505–523.

Yudkowsky, E. (2008). Artificial intelligence as a positive and negative factor in global risk. In: *Global Catastrophic Risks*, Oxford University Press, 308–345.

Zwitter, A. and Boisse-Despiaux, M. (2018). Blockchain for humanitarian action and development aid. *Journal of International Humanitarian Action*, 3(1), 1–14.

Index

9 783119 142168